Praise for *The Object Constraint Language, Second Edition*

"In this thoroughly revised edition, Jos and Anneke offer a concise, pragmatic, and pedagogic explanation of the Object Constraint Language (OCL) and its different applications. Their discussion of OCL's potential role in Model Driven Architecture (MDA) is timely and offers great insight into the way that UML can be taken to the next level of automated software development practice. I highly recommend this book to anyone who is looking to get the most out of UML."

> — Shane Sendall, PhD
> Senior Researcher
> Swiss Federal Institute of Technology, Lausanne

"MDA promises a revolution in the way we develop software. This book is essential reading for anyone intending to adopt MDA technology."

> — Tony Clark, PhD
> King's College, London

"Through examples, Jos and Anneke demonstrate the power and intuitiveness of OCL, and the key role that this language plays in implementing and promoting MDA. The theme, structure, contents, and, not lastly, the clarity of explanations recommend this book as the best advocate for learning, using, and promoting OCL, UML, and MDA. I am sure that this work will contribute in a significant manner to the development and widespread use of new software technologies."

> — Dan Chiorean
> Head of the Computer Science Research Laboratory
> Babes-Bolyai University, Cluj

D1584480

The Object Constraint Language
Second Edition

Getting Your Models Ready for MDA

Jos Warmer
Anneke Kleppe

✦✦ Addison-Wesley

Boston • San Francisco • New York • Toronto • Montreal
London • Munich • Paris • Madrid
Capetown • Sydney • Tokyo • Singapore • Mexico City

The publisher offers discounts on this book when ordered in quantity for bulk purchases and special sales. For more information, please contact:

> U.S. Corporate and Government Sales
> (800) 382-3419
> corpsales@pearsontechgroup.com

For sales outside of the U.S., please contact:

> International Sales
> (317) 581-3793
> international@pearsontechgroup.com

Library of Congress Cataloging-in-Publication Data

Warmer, Jos B.
   The object constraint language : getting your models ready for MDA / Jos Warmer, Anneke Kleppe.
     p. cm.
  Includes bibliographical references and index.
  ISBN 0-321-17936-6
   1. Object-oriented methods (Computer science) 2. UML (Computer science) I. Kleppe, Anneke G. II. Title.

QA76.9.O35W35 2003
005.1'17--dc22   2003057724

ISBN 0321179366
Text printed on recycled paper
1 2 3 4 5 6 7 8 9 10-CRS-0706050403
First printing, August 2003

Contents

Chapter 3
Building Models with OCL 37

Chapter 5
Using OCL for MDA 93

Part 2
Reference Manual 105

Chapter 6
The Context of OCL Expressions. 107

Appendix C
A Business Modeling Syntax for OCL

Appendix D
Example Implementation

Appendix E
Differences Between OCL Versions 1.1 and 2.0

Bibliography

Index

List of Figures

List of Tables

Foreword to the First Edition

For many years there has been a branch of computer science concerned with using formal logical languages to give precise and unambiguous descriptions of things. As an academic in the 1970s and 1980s I was very interested in such languages, for example Z and Larch. Unravelling the meaning of a statement in one of these languages is sometimes like a complex jigsaw puzzle, but once the unravelling is done the meaning is always crystal-clear and unambiguous. As I moved into the world of object-oriented methods I found a different way of specifying, using diagrams. With diagrams, the meaning is quite obvious, because once you understand how the basic elements of the diagram fit together, the meaning literally stares you in the face.

But there are many subtleties and nuances of meaning that diagrams cannot convey by themselves: uniqueness, derivation, limits, constraints, etc. So it occurred to me that from a modelling perspective a carefully designed combination of diagrammatic and formal languages would offer the best of both worlds. Armed with this realisation I worked during the early 1990s with John Daniels to create Syntropy, an object-oriented modelling language which combined the diagrammatic simplicity and clarity of OMT with the formality of a subset of Z.

Object Constraint Language (OCL) was first developed in 1995 during a business modelling project within IBM in which both Jos Warmer and I were involved, working in IBM's Object Technology Practice. This project was heavily influenced by Syntropy ideas. But unlike in Syntropy there is no use in OCL of unfamiliar mathematical symbols. OCL was very carefully designed to be both formal and simple: its syntax is very straightforward and can be picked up in a few minutes by anybody reasonably familiar with modelling or programming concepts.

During 1996 Jos and I became involved in the Object Management Group's efforts to standardize on a language for object-oriented analysis and design. I led IBM's contribution to this process, and together with ObjecTime Limited we wrote a proposal which emphasised simplicity and precision. Our goal all along was to collaborate with the other submitters to produce an overall standard containing the right elements in the right balance. OCL was a fundamental aspect of this proposal.

The leading proposal was UML (Unified Modeling Language) from Rational Software Corporation and its partners. UML, which combined ideas from its three authors Grady Booch, Ivar Jacobson, and James Rumbaugh, focused primarily on the diagrammatic elements and gave meaning to those elements through English text. As the submissions were combined, OCL was used to give added precision to the definition of UML; in addition OCL became part of the standard and thus available to modellers to express those additional nuances of meaning which just the diagrams cannot represent. This is a very important addition to the standard language of object-oriented modelling.

Jos Warmer and Anneke Kleppe's book is a crucial addition to the object-oriented modeling literature. I've greatly enjoyed working with Jos on the development of OCL over the past few years, and he and Anneke have done a first-class job in this book of explaining OCL and making it accessible to modellers. They have focused on the important aspects and illustrated the concepts with plenty of simple examples. Even for those with no experience of formal methods this book is an excellent place to learn how to add precision and detail to your models.

October 1998, Steve Cook

Foreword to the Second Edition

I first came in contact with model-driven architecture in 1998 when I started with a company called BoldSoft, which is now a part of Borland. Of course, at that time the term Model Driven Architecture (MDA) was not yet coined by the Object Management Group, and what we were doing does not directly match the MDA terminology as it is defined today in terms of Platform Independent Models and Platform Specific Models.

This was also my first contact with OCL. When I came to BoldSoft, they explained to me about their product, a framework for building applications based on UML models, and then they said, "Oh, and we have implemented this little language," and they handed me *The Object Constraint Language: Precise Modeling with UML* by Jos Warmer and Anneke Kleppe, the book for which what you are holding in your hands right now is the second edition.

I would say that the reasons why OCL is a successful language are threefold. First, it is small. There is only a handful of simple concepts to grasp: you access an attribute, call a function, or select objects from a collection. Second, it is compact, yet powerful. You can write short and to-the-point expressions that "do a lot." Third, and perhaps most important, it has the feel of an ordinary object-oriented programming language. It has no mathematical symbols or advanced theoretical concepts, but a syntax and structure that is readily accessible to most people with some experience in software development.

I have been able to observe the success of OCL firsthand at BoldSoft. The OCL implementation is one of the features of our framework that has received the most praise from our customers. Many of them have become devoted OCL fans. They appreciate that it is easy to learn, but mostly they appreciate that it simplifies their work. They are software developers, and they know how much programming would be required in an ordinary programming language to do the same thing as one small OCL expression.

During the last couple of years, I have had the pleasure of working with Jos and Anneke in the development of the new version of the standard for OCL, OCL 2.0. This work has focused on strengthening the semantic foundation for OCL, and adding a few well-chosen capabilities to enhance OCL's expressive power, to make it ready to deliver its part of the MDA promise. Therefore, it is fitting that the new version of the standard should be accompanied by a new edition of Jos' and Anneke's OCL book.

It is a comprehensive book. Not only does it cover the OCL language itself, both with easy-to-follow examples and in-depth explanations of every language element, it also puts the language into context and shows how and where to use OCL. The book contains numerous tips and tricks for modeling with OCL, and it paints the broader picture of how OCL fits into the Model Driven Architecture, and UML modeling in general. There can be no doubt that it will be the definitive work on OCL for many years to come.

Anders Ivner

Preface and Introduction

In November 1997, the Object Management Group (OMG) set a standard for object-oriented analysis and design facilities. The standard, known as the Unified Modeling Language (UML), includes model diagrams, their semantics, and an interchange format between CASE tools. Within UML, the Object Constraint Language (OCL) is the standard for specifying expressions that add vital information to object-oriented models and other object modeling artifacts.

In UML version 1.1, this information was thought to be limited to constraints, where a *constraint* is defined as a restriction on one or more values of (part of) an object-oriented model or system. In UML version 2, the understanding is that far more additional information should be included in a model than constraints alone. Defining queries, referencing values, or stating conditions and business rules in a model are all done by writing expressions, i.e., these are all expressed in OCL.

OCL evolved from an expression language in the Syntropy method through a business modeling language used within IBM until it was included in UML in 1997. At that point in time, it received its current name. This name is now well established, so it would not be expedient to change it to, for instance, *Object Expression Language*, although this name would currently be more appropriate.

OCL has been used as an expression language for object-oriented modeling during the last six years. Today, a large number of tools support the language. Since OCL was first conceived, there have been many changes and additions to the language. Lately, this has led to a new version of OCL, version 2, to accompany the new version of UML. OCL version 2 is formally defined in the *Object Constraint Language Specification* [OCL03]. This book explains all features of this version of OCL.

Recently, the OMG has launched an initiative called the Model Driven Architecture (MDA). The essence of the MDA approach is that models form the basis of software development. In order to work with this architecture one needs good, solid, consistent, and coherent models. Using the combination of UML and OCL, you can build such models.

In the many books that have been published on the subject of UML, its expression language has not received the attention it deserves. The first aim of this book is to fill this gap and to explain UML's expression language, which supports the task of modeling object-oriented software as much as the UML diagrams. The second aim of this book is to introduce OCL version 2 to a wider audience. Not everyone is pleased with reading a formal standard; the information should be available in a more accessible form. The last aim of this book is to explain why using OCL is essential to the application of MDA. Without OCL and the languages, transformations, and so on that are all enabled by OCL, application of the MDA is bound to fail.

WHO SHOULD READ THIS BOOK

The book is meant to be a textbook and reference manual for practitioners of object technology who need more precise modeling. This certainly includes persons who want to apply MDA principles. These users will want to use OCL in their analysis and design tasks, most probably within the context of UML, but potentially with other graphical object modeling languages.

This book assumes that you have general knowledge of object-oriented modeling, preferably UML. If you lack this knowledge, there are many books on UML that you can read first.

HOW THIS BOOK SHOULD BE USED

Part 1 of this book explains how OCL can be put to use. Anyone unfamiliar with OCL should read this part. It provides an introduction to the Model Driven Architecture and the key role OCL plays in that framework. In this part, OCL is explained in a relatively informal way, mostly by example. It also offers hints and tips on how to build models using OCL, and how to implement these models.

Part 2 constitutes a reference guide that describes the OCL language completely. If you are already familiar with OCL, you can find everything you want to know about the new version of OCL in this part.

Appendix A is a reference on the terminology used in this book. Appendix B is a reference on the syntax of the language. Finally, Appendix C would be of interest to people who feel that the official (concrete) syntax of OCL could be improved. It offers an example of a different syntax, called Business Modeling Syntax, that may be substituted for the official syntax.

TYPEFACE CONVENTIONS

This book uses the following typeface conventions:

- All OCL expressions and context definitions are printed in a `monospaced font`.

- All OCL keywords are printed in a `monospaced bold font`.

- At the first introduction or definition of a term, the term is shown in *italics*.

- All references to classes, attributes, and other elements of a UML diagram are shown in *italics*.

- All references to types start with a capital letter and are shown in *italics*. All references to instances of that type start with a lowercase letter. For instance, in the sentence "The value of a boolean expression is an instance of type *Boolean*," the first occurrence of the word boolean refers to a value, the second refers to the type.

INFORMATION ON RELATED SUBJECTS

The text of the UML and OCL standards is freely available from the OMG Web site (www.omg.org). Recent information on OCL can be found on the Klasse Objecten Web site: www.klasse.nl/ocl/. In addition, several available tools can translate OCL to code. Because the tool market is rapidly changing, we do not provide a list of tools in this book; it would be outdated quickly. Instead, on the aforementioned Web site you can find an up-to-date list of currently available tools.

ACKNOWLEDGMENTS

Although the cover of any book features only the names of the authors, a book is always the result of the blood, sweat, and tears of many people. For their efforts in reviewing the first edition this book, we would like to thank Balbir Barn, Steve Cook, Wilfried van Hulzen, John Hogg, Jim Odell, and Cor Warmer. Special thanks go to Heidi Kuehn, who did a great job polishing our English.

Acknowledgments for their contributions to the first version of OCL must undoubtedly go to the following:

- The IBM team that developed the first version of OCL: Mark Skipper, Anna Karatza, Aldo Eisma, Steve Cook, and Jos Warmer.
- The joint submission team from IBM and ObjecTime. The ObjecTime team was composed of John Hogg, Bran Selic, and Garth Gullekson; and the IBM team consisted of Steve Cook, Dipayan Gangopadhyay, Mike Meier, Subrata Mitra, and Jos Warmer. On an individual basis, Marc Saaltink, Alan Wills, and Anneke Kleppe also contributed.
- The UML 1.1 team, especially the semi-formal subgroup of the UML core team: Guus Ramackers, Gunnar Overgaard, and Jos Warmer.
- Several people who influenced OCL during this period, most notably Desmond D'Souza, Alan Wills, Steve Cook, John Hogg, and James Rumbaugh.
- The many persons who gave their feedback on the earlier versions of OCL.

The following people are acknowledged for their contribution to the further development of OCL, that concluded in version 2.0 of the OMG standard:

- The members of the OCL 2.0 submission team: Tony Clark, Anders Ivner, Jonas Högström, Martin Gogolla, Mark Richters, Heinrich Hußmann, Steffen Zschaler, Simon Johnston, Anneke Kleppe, and Jos Warmer.
- The participants of the OCL workshops during the UML 2000, and UML 2001 conferences.
- People who made us aware of mistakes in the earlier edition of this book.

We would also like to thank all our teachers, colleagues, clients, and friends who in the past two decades made us aware of the need for a practical form of formalism in software development. Coming from a theoretical background (mathematics and theoretical computer science), we have always found sound formalisms appealing, but very early in our careers we decided that writing a two-page "proof" for five lines of code is not the right way to improve our software. We have been searching ever since for a way to combine our love for sound and complete formalisms with our sense of practicality. We hope and expect that OCL will prove to be just that: a practical formalism.

Anneke Kleppe and Jos Warmer

June 2003, Soest, Netherlands

Part 1

User Manual

Chapter 1

MDA and the Use of OCL

This chapter explains why it is important to create models that contain as much information about the system as possible, especially when working within the Model Driven Architecture. Because the Model Driven Architecture itself is fairly new, a short introduction to this framework is given. Most important, this chapter states why OCL is a vital and necessary element in the Model Driven Architecture.

1.1 INTRODUCING OCL

The *Object Constraint Language* (OCL) is a modeling language with which you can build software models. It is defined as a standard "add-on" to the Unified Modeling Language (UML), the Object Management Group (OMG) standard for object-oriented analysis and design. Every expression written in OCL relies on the types (i.e., the classes, interfaces, and so on) that are defined in the UML diagrams. The use of OCL therefore includes the use of at least some aspects of UML.

Expressions written in OCL add vital information to object-oriented models and other object modeling artifacts. This information often cannot be expressed in a diagram. In UML 1.1, this information was thought to be limited to constraints, where a *constraint* is defined as a restriction on one or more values of (part of) an object-oriented model or system. In UML 2, the understanding is that far more additional information should be included in a model than constraints alone. Defining queries, referencing values, or stating conditions and business rules in a model are all accomplished by writing expressions. OCL is the standard language in which these expressions can be written in a clear and unambiguous manner.

Recently, a new version of OCL, version 2.0, has been formally defined in the *Object Constraint Language Specification* [OCL03] and as such it has been adopted by the OMG. This book explains this version of OCL and how it can be put to use in software development.

There is a strong relationship between all OMG standards. The most recent OMG initiative is the Model Driven Architecture (MDA). The essence of the MDA approach is that models are the basis for software development. Therefore, models should be good, solid, consistent, and coherent. Using the combination of UML and OCL, you can build such models.

1.2 MODEL DRIVEN ARCHITECTURE

The Model Driven Architecture (MDA) is gradually becoming an important aspect of software development. Many tools are, or at least claim to be, MDA-compliant, but what exactly is MDA?

MDA is a framework being built under supervision of the Object Management Group (OMG). It defines how models defined in one language can be transformed into models in other languages. An example of a transformation is the generation of a database schema from a UML model, UML being the source language and SQL being the target language. Source code is also considered to be a model. Code generation from a UML model is therefore another form of transformation.

This section presents a brief introduction to MDA; it is by no means complete. You can find more information about MDA on the OMG Web site and in a number of books; for example, see *MDA Explained, The Model Driven Architecture: Practice and Promise,* by the same authors [Kleppe03].

1.2.1 PIMs and PSMs

Key to MDA is the importance of models in the software development process. Within MDA, the software development process is driven by the activity of modeling your software system. The MDA process is divided into three steps:

1. Build a model with a high level of abstraction, which is independent of any implementation technology. This is called a *Platform Independent Model* (PIM).
2. Transform the PIM into one or more models that are tailored to specify your system in terms of the implementation constructs that are available in one specific implementation technology; e.g., a database model or an EJB (Enterprise Java Beans) model. These models are called *Platform Specific Models* (PSMs).
3. Transform the PSMs to code.

Because a PSM fits its technology very closely, the last transformation is straightforward. The complex step is the one in which a PIM is transformed to a PSM. The relationships between PIM, PSM, source code, and the transformations between them, are depicted in Figure 1-1.

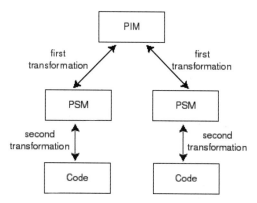

Figure 1-1 *The relationship between PIM, PSM, and code*

1.2.2 Automation of Transformations

Another key element of MDA is that the transformations are executed by tools. Many tools have been able to transform a platform-specific model to code; there is nothing new about that. What's new is that the transformation from PIM to PSM is automated as well. This is where the obvious benefits of MDA lie. Anyone who has been around a while in the business of software development knows how much time is spent on tasks that are more or less routine. For example, building a database model from an object-oriented design, or building a COM (Common Object Model) component model or an EJB component model from another high-level design. The MDA goal is to automate the cumbersome and laborious part of software development.

1.2.3 MDA Building Blocks

The MDA framework consists of a number of highly related parts. To understand the framework, you must understand both the individual parts and their mutual relationships. Therefore, let's take a closer look at each of the parts of the MDA framework: the models, the modeling languages, the transformation tools, and the transformation definitions, which are depicted in Figure 1-2.

Models

The first and foremost element of MDA is formed by models—high-level models (PIMs) and low-level models (PSMs). The whole idea of MDA is that a PIM can be transformed into more than one PSM, each suited for different target technologies. If the PIM were to reflect design decisions made with only one of the target technologies in mind, it could not be transformed into a PSM based on a different target technology; the PIMs must truly be independent of any implementation technology.

A PSM, conversely, must closely reflect the concepts and constructs used in the corresponding technology. In a PSM targeted at databases, for instance, the table, column, and foreign key concepts should be clearly recognizable. The close relationship between the PSM and its technology ensures that the transformation to code will be efficient and effective.

All models, both PSM and PIM, should be consistent and precise, and contain as much information as possible about the system. This is where OCL can be helpful, because UML diagrams alone do not typically provide enough information.

Modeling Languages

Modeling languages form another element of the MDA framework. Because both PIMs and PSMs are transformed automatically, they should be written in a standard, well-defined modeling language that can be processed by automated tools. Nevertheless, the PIMs are written by hand. Before a system is built, only humans know what it must do. Therefore, PIMs must be written to be understood and corrected by other humans. This places high demands on the modeling language used for PIMs. It must be understood by both humans and machines.

The PSMs, however, will be generated, and the PSM needs to be understood only by automated tools and by experts in that specific technology. The demands on the languages used for specifying PSMs are relatively lower than those on the language for PIMs. Currently, a number of so-called profiles for UML define UML-like languages for specific technologies, e.g., the EJB profile [EJB01].

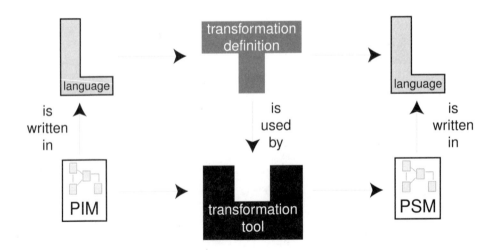

Figure 1-2 *The MDA Framework*

Transformation Tools

There is a growing market of transformation tools. These tools implement the central part of the MDA approach, thus automating a substantial portion of the software development process. Many tools implement the PSM-to-code transformation. Currently, only a few implement the execution of the transformation definitions from PIM to PSM. Most of the PIM-to-PSM tools are combined with a PSM-to-code component. These tools should offer users the flexibility to tune the transformation to their specific needs.

Transformation Definitions

Another vital part of the MDA framework is formed by the definitions of how a PIM is to be transformed to a specific PSM, and how a PSM is to be transformed into code. Transformation definitions are separated from the tools that will execute them, in order to re-use them, even with different tools. It is not worthwhile to build a transformation definition for onetime use. It is far more effective when a transformation can be executed repeatedly on any PIM or PSM written in a specific language.

Some of the transformation definitions will be user-defined, that is, written by the developers that work according to the MDA process. Preferably, transformation definitions would be in the public domain, perhaps even standardized, and tuneable to the individual needs of its users. Some tool vendors have developed their own transformation definitions, which unfortunately usually cannot be adapted by users because their use is not transparent, but hidden in the functionality of the tools.

1.2.4 MDA Benefits

This section describes some of the advantages of MDA:

1. *Portability,* increasing application re-use and reducing the cost and complexity of application development and management, now and in the future. MDA brings us portability and platform independency because the PIM is indeed platform independent and can be used to generate several PSMs for different platforms.
2. *Productivity,* by enabling developers, designers, and system administrators to use languages and concepts they are comfortable with, while still supporting seamless communication and integration across the teams. A productivity gain can be achieved by using tools that fully automate the generation of code from a PSM, and even more when the generation of a PSM from a PIM is automated as well.
3. *Cross-platform interoperability,* using rigorous methods to guarantee that standards based on multiple implementation technologies all implement identical business functions. The promise of cross-platform interoperability can be ful-

filled by tools that not only generate PSMs, but also the bridges between them, and possibly to other platforms as well.

4. *Easier maintenance and documentation*, as MDA implies that much of the information about the application must be incorporated in the PIM. It also implies that building a PIM takes less effort than writing code.

1.2.5 The Silver Bullet?

When explaining the MDA to software developers, we often get a skeptical response: "This can never work. You cannot generate a complete working program from a model. You will always need to adjust the code." Is MDA just promising another silver bullet?

We believe that MDA may change the future of software development radically. One argument for this is that although MDA is still in its infancy, you can today achieve great gains in productivity, portability, interoperability, and maintenance efforts by applying MDA using a good transformation tool. Therefore, MDA is, and will continue to be, used. A second argument comes from the history of computing.

In the early 1960s, our industry was in the middle of a revolution. The use of existing assembly languages was replaced with the use of procedural languages. There was a lot of skepticism in those days too, and not without reason. The first compilers were not very good. The Algol programming language, for instance, offered the potential to the programmer to give hints to the compiler about how to translate a piece of code. Many programmers were concerned that the generated assembler code would be far less efficient than handwriting the assembler code themselves. Many could not believe that compilers would become proficient enough to stop worrying about this.

To a certain extent the skeptics were right. You lost efficiency and speed, and you could not program all the assembler tricks in a procedural language. However, the advantages of procedural languages became increasingly obvious. Using higher level languages, you can write more complex software much faster, and the resulting code is much easier to maintain. At the same time, better compiler technology diminished the disadvantages. The generated assembler code became more efficient. Today, we accept the fact that we should not program our systems in assembler. Indeed, anyone planning to write a new customer relationship management system in assembler today would be declared insane.

What MDA brings us is another revolution of the same kind. Eventually, PIMs can be *compiled* (read: transformed) into PSMs, which are *compiled* into procedural language code (which itself is compiled into assembly or raw machine code). The PIM-to-PSM *compilers* (read: transformation tools) will not be very efficient for some years to come. Their users will need to provide hints about how to transform parts of a model. Eventually however, the advantage of working on a higher level of abstraction will become clear to everyone in the business.

Concluding, we can say that although MDA is still in its infancy, it shows the potential to radically change the way we develop software. We are likely witnessing the birth of a paradigm shift; and in the near future, software development will shift its focus from code to models.

1.3 MODELING MATURITY LEVELS

Within the MDA process, the focus of software development will be on producing a high level model of the system. Currently, many people use UML or another modeling language during software development. However, they all use this standard language in very different ways. To create some order and transparency in working with models, we introduce the modeling maturity levels (MMLs). These levels can be compared to the CMM levels [CMM95]. They indicate what role models play in your software development process, and the direction you need to take to improve this process.

Traditionally, there has been a gap between the model and the system. The model is used as a plan, as brainstorm material, or as documentation, but the system is the real thing. Often, the detailed software code strays a long way from the original model. On every modeling maturity level, this gap is reduced, as shown in Figure 1-3, where the right side represents the actual system and the left side represents the model of the system.

As one climbs to a higher maturity level, the term *programming* gets a new meaning. At a higher maturity level, modeling and programming become almost the same. To be clear in the descriptions of each level, we use the word *coding* to mean the final transformation of all knowledge and decisions about the application—in whatever form that may be—to executable programming language code. Correspondingly, we speak of the *coder* instead of the *programmer*.

1.3.1 Level 0: No Specification

At the lowest level, the specification of the software is in the heads of the developers only. This level is common among nonprofessional software developers. One simply gets an idea about what to develop, and talks about it without ever writing anything down. The characteristics of this level are as follows:

- There are often conflicting views among developers, and between developers and users.
- This manner of working is suitable for small applications; larger and more complex applications need some form of design before coding.
- It is impossible to understand the code if the coders leave (and they always do).
- Many choices are made by the coders in an ad hoc fashion.

1.3.2 Level 1: Textual

At modeling maturity level 1, the specification of the software is written down in one or more natural language documents. These may be more or less formal, using numbering for every requirement or every system function or not, large or

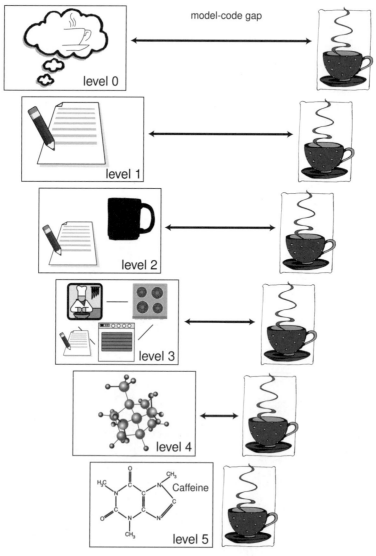

Figure 1-3 *The Modeling Maturity Levels bridging the model-code gap*

small, an overview or very detailed, depending on taste. This is the lowest level of professional software development. The characteristics of this level are as follows:

- The specification is ambiguous, because natural language inherently is.
- The coder makes business decisions based on his or her personal interpretation of the text(s).
- It is impossible to keep the specification up to date after changing the code.

1.3.3 Level 2: Text with Diagrams

At modeling maturity level 2, the specification of the software is provided by one or more natural language documents augmented with several high-level diagrams to explain the overall architecture and/or some complex details. The characteristics of this level are as follows:

- The text still specifies the system, but it is easier to understand because of the diagrams.
- All characteristics of level 1 are still present.

1.3.4 Level 3: Models with Text

A set of models, i.e., either diagrams or text with a very specific and well-defined meaning, forms the specification of the software at modeling maturity level 3. Additional natural language text explains the background and motivation of the models, and fills in many details, but the models are the most important part of the design/analysis deliverables. The characteristics of this level are as follows:

- The diagrams or formal texts are real representations of the software.
- The transition of model to code is mostly manual.
- It is still impossible (or very difficult) to keep the specification up to date after changing the code.
- The coder still makes business decisions, but these have less influence on the architecture of the system.

1.3.5 Level 4: Precise Models

A model, meaning a consistent and coherent set of texts and/or diagrams with a very specific and well-defined meaning, specifies the software at modeling maturity level 4. Here, too, natural language text is used to add comments that explain the background and motivation of the model. The models at this level are precise enough to have a direct link with the actual code. However, they have a different level of abstraction. A model is more than the concepts of some programming language depicted in diagrams. Level 4 is the level at which the Model Driven Architecture is targeted. At this level:

- Coders do not make business decisions anymore.

- Keeping models and code up to date is essential and easy.
- Iterative and incremental development are facilitated by the direct transformation from model to code.

1.3.6 Level 5: Models Only

A level 5 model is a complete, consistent, detailed, and precise description of the system. At level 5, the models are good enough to enable complete code-generation. No adjustments need to be made to the resulting code. Software developers can rely on the model-to-code generation in the same way coders today rely on their compilers. The generated code will be invisible to the developer; there is no need to look into it. The language in which the models are written has become the next-generation programming language. Certainly, some text is still present in the model, but its function is equal to comments in source code.

Note that this level has not been realized yet anywhere in the world. This is future technology, unfortunately. Still, it is good to recognize what our ultimate goal is.

1.4 BUILDING BETTER MODELS

In order to apply the MDA process, models on maturity level 4 are neccessary. This is the first level at which a model is more than just paper. At level 4, the models are precise enough to have a direct link with the source code. If you want to be able to transform a model from PIM through a PSM to code, this precision is necessary.

How do you build level 4 models? In Section 1.1, we already mentioned that the best choice for a modeling language for building PIMs is UML in combination with OCL. By specifying your model in a combination of the UML and OCL languages, you can improve the quality of your models.

1.4.1 Why Combine UML and OCL?

Modeling, especially software modeling, has traditionally been a synonym for producing diagrams. Most models consist of a number of "bubbles and arrows" pictures and some accompanying text. The information conveyed by such a model has a tendency to be incomplete, informal, imprecise, and sometimes even inconsistent.

Many of the flaws in the model are caused by the limitations of the diagrams being used. A diagram simply cannot express the statements that should be part of a thorough specification. For instance, in the UML model shown in Figure 1-4, an association between class *Flight* and class *Person*, indicating that a certain group of persons are the passengers on a flight, will have multiplicity many (0..*)

on the side of the *Person* class. This means that the number of passengers is unlimited. In reality, the number of passengers will be restricted to the number of seats on the airplane that is associated with the flight. It is impossible to express this restriction in the diagram. In this example, the correct way to specify the multiplicity is to add to the diagram the following OCL constraint:

```
context Flight
inv: passengers->size() <= plane.numberOfSeats
```

Expressions written in a precise, mathematically based language like OCL offer a number of benefits over the use of diagrams to specify a (business or software) system. For example, these expressions cannot be interpreted differently by different people, e.g., an analyst and a programmer. They are unambiguous and make the model more precise and more detailed. These expressions can be checked by automated tools to ensure that they are correct and consistent with other elements of the model. Code generation becomes much more powerfull.

However, a model written in a language that uses an expression representation alone is often not easily understood. For example, while source code can be regarded as the ultimate model of the software, most people prefer a diagrammatic model in their encounters with the system. The good thing about "bubbles and arrows" pictures is that their intended meaning is easy to grasp.

The combination of UML and OCL offers the best of both worlds to the software developer. A large number of different diagrams, together with expressions written in OCL, can be used to specify models. Note that to obtain a complete model, both the diagrams and OCL expressions are necessary. Without OCL expressions, the model would be severely underspecified; without the UML diagrams, the OCL expressions would refer to non-existing model elements, as there is no way in OCL to specify classes and associations. Only when we combine the diagrams and the constraints can we completely specify the model.

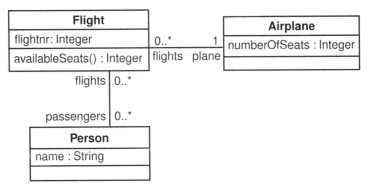

Figure 1-4 *A model expressed in a diagram*

1.4.2 Value Added by OCL

Still not convinced that using OCL adds value to the use of UML alone? The diagram in Figure 1-5 shows another example, which contains three classes: *Person*, *House*, and *Mortgage*, and their associations. Any human reader of the model will undoubtedly assume that a number of rules must apply to this model.

1. A person may have a mortgage on a house only if that house is owned by him- or herself; one cannot obtain a mortgage on the house of one's neighbor or friend.
2. The start date for any mortgage must be before the end date.
3. The social security number of all persons must be unique.
4. A new mortgage will be allowed only when the person's income is sufficient.
5. A new mortgage will be allowed only when the countervalue of the house is sufficient.

The diagram does not show this information; nor is there any way in which the diagrams might express these rules. If these rules are not documented, different readers might make different assumptions, which will lead to an incorrect understanding, and an incorrect implementation of the system. Writing these rules in English, as we have done above, isn't enough either. By definition, English text is ambiguous and very easy to interpret in different ways. The same problem of misunderstanding and incorrect implementation remains.

Only by augmenting the model with the OCL expressions for these rules can a complete and precise description of the "mortgage system" be obtained. OCL is unambigous and the rules cannot be misunderstood. The rules in OCL are as follows:

```
context Mortgage
inv: security.owner = borrower

context Mortgage
inv: startDate < endDate

context Person
inv: Person::allInstances()->isUnique(socSecNr)

context Person::getMortgage(sum : Money, security : House)
pre: self.mortgages.monthlyPayment->sum() <= self.salary * 0.30

context Person::getMortgage(sum : Money, security : House)
pre: security.value >= security.mortgages.principal->sum()
```

It is essential to include these rules as OCL expressions in the model for a number of reasons. As stated earlier, no misunderstanding occurs when humans read the model. Errors are therefore found in an early stage of development, when fixing a

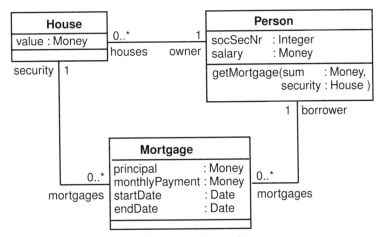

Figure 1-5 *The "mortgage system" expressed in a diagram*

fault is relatively cheap. The intended meaning of the analyst who builds the model is clear to the programmers who will implement the model.

When the model is not read by humans, but instead is used as input to an automated system, the use of OCL becomes even more important. Tools can be used for generating simulations and tests, for checking consistency, for generating derived models in other languages using MDA transformations, for generating code, and so on. This type of work most people would gladly leave to a computer, if it would and could be done properly.

However, automating this work is only possible when the model itself contains all of the information needed. A computerized tool cannot interpret English rules. The rules written in OCL include all the necessary information for automated MDA tools. This way, implementation is faster and more efficient than by hand, and there is a guaranteed consistency between the model in UML/OCL and the generated artifacts. The level of maturity of the software development process as a whole is raised.

1.5 CHARACTERISTICS OF OCL

In the previous section, we saw that even a simple three-class model needs much additional information in OCL to make it complete, consistent, and unambiguous. If you had only the UML diagram, many open questions would remain. It is very likely that a system built based on the diagram alone will be incorrect. It is clear that OCL is a vital language for building better models. In the next section, we will take a closer look at some of the characteristics of OCL.

1.5.1 Both Query and Constraint Language

In UML 1.1, OCL was a language to express constraints on the elements given in the diagrams of the model. In the introduction to this book, we already defined a constraint as follows:

> *A constraint is a restriction on one or more values of (part of) an object-oriented model or system.*

What this means is that although the diagrams in the model state that certain objects or data values may be present in the modeled system, these values are valid only if the condition specified by the constraint holds. For example, the diagram in Figure 1-4 tells us that flights may have any number of passengers, but the constraint restricts the flights to those for which the number of passengers is equal to or less than the number of seats on the plane. Flights for which the condition does not hold are not valid in the specified system.

In UML 2, OCL can be used to write not only constraints, but any expression on the elements in the diagram. Every OCL expression indicates a value or object within the system. For example, the expression *1+3* is a valid OCL expression of type *Integer*, which represents the integer value 4. When the value of an expression is of *Boolean* type, it may be used as a constraint. Therefore, the possibilities that the language offers have grown considerably.

OCL expressions can be used anywhere in the model to indicate a value. A value can be a simple value, such as an integer, but it may also be a reference to an object, a collection of values, or a collection of references to objects. An OCL expression can represent, e.g., a boolean value used as a condition in a statechart, or a message in an interaction diagram. An OCL expression can be used to refer to a specific object in an interaction or object diagram. The next expression, for example, defines the body of the operation *availableSeats()* of the class *Flight*:

```
context Flight::availableSeats() : Integer
body: plane.numberOfSeats - passengers->size()
```

Other examples of using OCL expressions include the definition of the derivation of a derived attribute or association (explained in Section 3.3.8), or the specification of the initial value of attributes or associations (explained in Section 3.3.2).

Because an OCL expression can indicate any value or collection of values in a system, OCL has the same capabilities as SQL, as proved in [Akehurst01]. This is clearly illustrated by the fact that the body of a query operation can be completely specified by a single OCL expression. However, neither SQL nor OCL is a constraint language. OCL is a constraint and query language at the same time.

1.5.2 Mathematical Foundation, But No Mathematical Symbols

An outstanding characteristic of OCL is its mathematical foundation. It is based on mathematical set theory and predicate logic, and it has a formal mathematical semantics [Richters01]. The notation, however, does not use mathematical symbols. Experience with formal or mathematical notations have led to the following conclusion: The people who can use the notation can express things precisely and unambiguously, but very few people can really understand such a notation. Although it seems a good candidate for a precise, unambiguous notation, a mathematical notation is not suitable for a standard language that is to be widely used.

A modeling language needs the rigor and precision of mathematics, but the ease of use of natural language. These are conflicting requirements, so finding the right balance is essential. In OCL, this balance is found by using the mathematical concepts without the abracadabra of the mathematical notation. Instead of using mathematical symbols, OCL uses plain ascii words that express the same concept.

Especially in the context of MDA, where a model needs to be transformed automatically, the value of an unambiguous mathematical foundation for the PIM language is of great value. There can be no doubt as to what an OCL expression means, and different tools must understand the expressions in the same way.

The result is a precise, unambiguous language that should be easily read and written by all practitioners of object technology and by their customers, i.e., people who are not mathematicians or computer scientists. If you still do not like the syntax of OCL, you may define your own. The OCL specification allows anyone to define his or her own syntax. The only condition is that your syntax can be mapped to the language structures defined in the standard [OCL03]. Appendix C provides an example of a different syntax expressing the same underlying structures. This syntax is directed toward use by business modelers.

1.5.3 Strongly Typed Language

An essential characteristic of OCL is that it is a typed language. OCL expressions are used for modeling and specification purposes. Because most models are not executed directly, most OCL expressions will be written while no executable version of the system exists. However, it must be possible to check an OCL expression without having to produce an executable version of the model. As a typed language, OCL expressions can be checked during modeling, before execution. Thus, errors in the model can be removed at an early stage.

Many popular programming languages are typed languages as well. Java, Eiffel, C#, delphi, and so on all fall into this category.

1.5.4 Declarative Language

Another distinguishing feature is that OCL is a declarative language. In procedural languages, like programming languages, expressions are descriptions of the actions that must be performed. In a declarative language, an expression simply states *what* should be done, but now *how*. To ensure this, OCL expressions have no side effects; that is, evaluating an OCL expression does not change the state of the system. Declarative languages have several advantages over procedural languages.

The modeler can make decisions at a high level of abstraction, without going into detail about how something should be calculated. For example, the body expression of the operation *availableSeats()* in Section 1.5.1 clearly specifies what the operation should calculate. How this should be done is not stated; this will depend on the implementation strategy of the whole system. One option is the representation of associations in the code. How do we find all of the passengers on a *Flight*? A flight object could contain a collection of references to its passengers. Alternatively, a *Flight* has no direct reference to its passengers, but needs to search a *Passenger* table in a database to find its passengers. A third implementation strategy would be to add an additional attribute to *Flight*, containing the number of passengers. Care should be taken to update the value of this attribute whenever a *Passenger* books or cancels a *Flight*. The body-expression in OCL allows for all of these implementations, because it describes only the what, not the how. If a procedural language were used to specify the body of *availableSeats()*, it would have forced a specific implementation style, which is undesirable for a PIM-level model.

In making OCL a declarative language, the expressions in a UML model are lifted fully into the realm of pure modeling, without regard for the nitty-gritty details of the implementation and the implementation language. An expression specifies values at a high level of abstraction, while remaining 100 percent precise.

1.6 SUMMARY

OCL is a language that can express additional and neccesary information about the models and other artifacts used in object-oriented modeling, and should be used in conjunction with UML diagrammatic models.

Much more information can be included in the specification (the model) using the combination of OCL and UML than through the use of UML alone. As you have seen, even in very simple examples, many essential aspects of the system cannot be expressed in a UML diagram. This information can only be expressed in the form of OCL expressions.

The level of maturity of the software process is raised by building a UML/OCL combined model. Tools that simulate a system, generate tests or source code from a model, and tools that support MDA need more detailed and more precise models as input. The quality of the output of these tools depends largely on the quality of the model used as input.

Tools that generate tests and source code from UML/OCL make the development process more efficient. The time invested in developing the UML/OCL models is regained during the subsequent stages of development.

OCL is a precise, unambiguous language that is easy for people who are not mathematicians or computer scientists to understand. It doesn't use any mathematical symbols, while maintaining mathematical rigor in its definition. OCL is a typed language, because it must be possible to check an OCL expression included in a specification without having to produce an executable version of the model.

OCL is a declarative, side-effects-free language; that is, the state of a system does not change because of an OCL expression. More importantly, a modeler can specify in OCL exactly what is meant, without restricting the implementation of the system that is being modeled. This enables a UML/OCL model to be completely platform-independent.

Chapter 2

OCL By Example

The sample system specification in this chapter provides a short and informal introduction to OCL. A complete and rigorous description of OCL can be found in Part 2. After reading this chapter, you will be able to add simple OCL expressions to your own UML models.

2.1 THE "ROYAL AND LOYAL" SYSTEM EXAMPLE

As an example, we have modeled a computer system for a fictional company called Royal and Loyal (R&L). R&L handles loyalty programs for companies that offer their customers various kinds of bonuses. Often, the extras take the form of bonus points or air miles, but other bonuses are possible as well: reduced rates, a larger rental car for the same price as a standard rental car, extra or better service on an airline, and so on. Anything a company is willing to offer can be a service rendered in a loyalty program. Figure 2-1 shows the UML class model that R&L uses for most of its clients, which is a typical platform-independent model (PIM) within the context of MDA. It shows no dependency on whatever programming language that will be used to build the system.

The central class in the model is *LoyaltyProgram*. A system that administers a single loyalty program will contain only one instance of this class. In the case of R&L, many instances of this class will be present in the system. A company that offers its customers membership in a loyalty program is called a *ProgramPartner*. More than one company can enter the same program. In that case, customers who enter the loyalty program can profit from services rendered by any of the participating companies.

Every customer of a program partner can enter the loyalty program by filling in a form and obtaining a membership card. The objects of class *Customer* represent the persons who have entered the program. The membership card, represented by the class *CustomerCard*, is issued to one person. Card use is not checked, so a single card could be used for an entire family or business. Most loyalty pro-

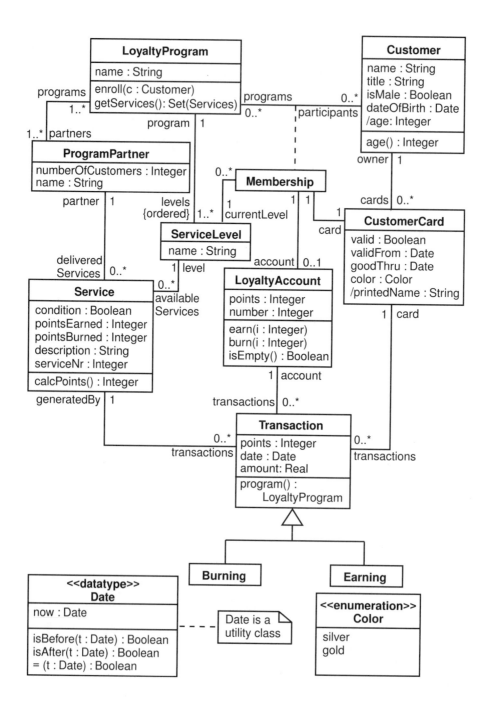

Figure 2-1 *The Royal and Loyal model*

grams allow customers to save bonus points. Each individual program partner decides when and how many bonus points are allotted for a certain purchase. Saved bonus points can be used to "buy" specific services from one of the program partners. To account for the bonus points that are saved by a customer, every membership can be associated with a *LoyaltyAccount*.

Various transactions on this account are possible. For example, the loyalty program "Silver and Gold" has four program partners: a supermarket, a line of gas stations, a car rental service, and an airline.

- At the supermarket, the customer can use bonus points to purchase items. The customer earns five bonus points for any regular purchase over the amount of $25.
- The gas stations offer a discount of 5 percent on every purchase.
- The car rental service offers 20 bonus points for every $100 spent.
- Customers can save bonus points for free flights with the airline company. For every flight that is paid for normally, the airline offers one bonus point for each 15 miles of flight.

In this situation, there are two types of transactions. First, there are transactions in which the customer obtains bonus points. In the model (see Figure 2-1), these transactions are represented by a subclass of *Transaction* called *Earning*. Second, there are transactions in which the customer spends bonus points. In the model, they are represented by instances of the *Burning* subclass of *Transaction*. The gas stations offer simple discounts but do not offer or accept bonus points. Because the turnover generated by the customers needs to be recorded, this is entered as two simultaneous transactions on the *LoyaltyAccount*, one *Earning* and one *Burning* for the same number of points.

Customers in the Silver and Gold program who make extensive use of the membership are rewarded with a higher level of service: the gold card. In addition to the regular services, customers who have a gold card are also offered the following additional services:

- Every two months, the supermarket offers an item that is completely free. The average value of the item is $25.
- The gas stations offer a discount of 10 percent on every purchase.
- The car rental service offers a larger car for the same price.
- The airline offers its gold card customers a business class seat for the economy class price.

Customers must meet at least one of the following conditions to get a gold card:

- Three sequential years of membership with an average annual turnover of $5,000
- One year of membership with a turnover of $15,000, where the turnover is the total turnover with all program partners

To administer different levels of service, the class *ServiceLevel* is introduced in the model. A service level is defined by the loyalty program and used for each membership.

R&L advertises the program and its conditions. It manages all customer data and transactions on the loyalty accounts. For this purpose, the program partners must inform R&L of all transactions on loyalty program membership cards. Each year, R&L sends new membership cards to all customers. When appropriate, R&L upgrades a membership card to a gold card. In this case, R&L sends the customer a new gold card along with information about the additional services offered, and R&L invalidates the old membership card.

The customer can withdraw from the program by sending a withdrawal form to R&L. Any remaining bonus points are canceled and the card is invalidated. R&L can invalidate a membership when the customer has not used the membership card for a certain period. For the Silver and Gold program, this period is one year.

We could tell you more about R&L, but the preceding description is sufficient for our purposes. The diagram in Figure 2-1 outlines the system model. Now it's time to add the neccessary details by adding some expressions and stating a number of useful and indispensable constraints.

2.2 ADDING EXTRA INFORMATION

The diagram in Figure 2-1 does not express all relevant information about the R&L system. The following sections provide examples of additional information that cannot be expressed in the diagram, but should be specified in OCL expressions.

2.2.1 Initial Values and Derivation Rules

A very basic addition to the diagram shown in Figure 2-1 is to include rules that state initial values for attributes and association ends. Initial value rules can be expressed very simply. First, you indicate the class that holds the attribute or association end. This class is called the *context*. Then you write the expression that states your initial value rule. For instance, a loyalty account will always be initialized with zero points, and a customer card will always be valid at the moment it is issued:

```
context LoyaltyAccount::points
init: 0

context CustomerCard::valid
init: true
```

Another small but indispensable part of the model is the specification for determining the value of derived elements. A model may contain derived attributes and derived associations. For both, a so-called *derivation rule* can be specified. Again, the context of the expression is the class that holds the attribute or association end. The expression after the context states the derivation rule. For instance, the derived attribute *printedName* of *CustomerCard* is determined based on the name and title of the card owner.

```
context CustomerCard::printedName
derive: owner.title.concat(' ').concat(owner.name)
```

In this example, the printedName is the concatenation of the title of the Customer who owns the card, its name, and a space between both strings (e.g., "Mr. Johnson").

2.2.2 Query Operations

Query operations are operations that do not change the state of the system; they simply return a value or set of values. The definition of the result of query operations cannot be given in a diagram. In OCL, this can be defined by writing a *body expression*. The operation name, parameters, and return type (its signature) are given as context. For instance, suppose the class *LoyaltyProgram* has a query operation *getServices*, which returns all services offered by all program partners in this program:

```
context LoyaltyProgram::getServices(): Set(Service)
body: partners.deliveredServices->asSet()
```

In this example, the association-end *deliveredServices* of *ProgramPartner* that holds a set of *Services* is used. For all instances of *ProgramPartner* that are associated with the *LoyaltyProgram* instance of which the operation *getServices* is called, these sets of *Services* are collected and combined into one set. This set is the result of the query operation.

In the *body* expression, the parameters of the operation may be used. For instance, suppose you need a more refined version of the *getServices* operation. This operation takes as a parameter a program partner object and returns the services delivered by the parameter object, if it is a partner in this program. In this case, the refined operation can be specified as follows:

```
context LoyaltyProgram::getServices(pp: ProgramPartner)
                                      : Set(Service)
body: if partners->includes(pp)
      then pp.deliveredServices
      else Set{}
      endif
```

The result of this query operation is the set of *Services* held by the parameter *pp*, or an empty set if the parameter instance of *ProgramPartner* is not a partner of the *LoyaltyProgram* for which the query operation is called.

Note that there is no difference between a derived attribute and a query operation that has no parameters, other than the notation. The query operation needs to be written using parentheses.

2.2.3 Defining New Attributes and Operations

Although most elements in the model are introduced in the UML diagrams, attributes and operations can be added to the model using an OCL expression. The context is the class to which the attribute or operation is added.

An attribute that has been defined in this manner is always a derived attribute. The expression that defines the attribute includes the name and type of the attribute, and the derivation rule. For instance, we might want to introduce an attribute called *turnover* in class *LoyaltyAccount*, which would sum the amount attributes of the transactions on the account. This attribute can be defined by the following expression. The part after the equal sign states the derivation rule for the new attribute:

```
context LoyaltyAccount
def: turnover : Real = transactions.amount->sum()
```

The derivation rule results in a single real number that is calculated by summing the value of the amount attribute in all transactions associated with the *LoyaltyAccount* instance that holds the newly defined attribute.

An operation that has been defined in an OCL expression is always a query operation. The expression after the equal sign states the body expression. For example, we might want to introduce the operation *getServicesByLevel* in the class *LoyaltyProgram*. This query operation returns the set of all delivered services for a certain level in a loyalty program:

```
context LoyaltyProgram
def: getServicesByLevel(levelName: String): Set(Service)
    = levels->select( name = levelName ).availableServices->asSet()
```

The result of the body expression is calculated from a selection of the levels associated with the instance of *LoyaltyProgram* for which the operation *getServicesByLevel* is called. It returns only the services available from the *ServiceLevel* whose name is equal to the parameter *levelName*. The reason for using the *asSet* operation is given in Section 2.4.2.

2.3 ADDING INVARIANTS

More information can be added to the model in the form of invariants. An *invariant* is a constraint that should be true for an object during its complete lifetime. Invariants often represent rules that should hold for the real-life objects after which the software objects are modeled.

2.3.1 Invariants on Attributes

A reasonable rule for every loyalty program of R&L would be to require that every customer who enters a loyalty program be of legal age. In the model, this means that the attribute *age* of every customer object must be equal to or greater than 18. This can be written as an invariant:

```
context Customer
inv ofAge: age >= 18
```

Invariants on one or more attributes of a class can be expressed in a very simple manner. The class to which the invariant refers is the context of the invariant. It is followed by a boolean expression that states your invariant. All attributes of the context class may be used in this invariant.

2.3.2 The Type of the Attribute Is a Class

When the attribute is not of a standard type, such as *Boolean* or *Integer*, but its type is a class itself, you can use the attributes or query operations defined on that class to write the invariant, using a dot notation. For example, the class *CustomerCard* contains two attributes *validFrom* and *goodThru* of type *Date*. A simple but useful invariant on these two date attributes states that *validFrom* should be earlier than *goodThru*:

```
context CustomerCard
inv checkDates: validFrom.isBefore(goodThru)
```

This invariant uses the operation *isBefore* in the *Date* class that checks whether the date in the parameter is later than the date object on which the operation is called. This results in a boolean value. Note that you may use only operations that do not change the value of any attributes; only the so-called query operations are allowed.

2.3.3 Invariants on Associated Objects

Invariants may also state rules for associated objects. The rule that every cardholder should be of age could also be stated as follows:

```
context CustomerCard
inv ofAge: owner.age >= 18
```

Stating an invariant on associated objects is done by using the *rolename* on the association to refer to the object on the other end. If the rolename is not present, you should use the name of the class. Note that the previous version of OCL required that the class name be written starting with a lowercase letter. In version 2, the name used should be identical to the name of the association class. Giving rolenames to each association end is preferred. Using rolenames to traverse an association to get to the corresponding instances is called *navigation*.

Finding the right context for an invariant can sometimes be challenging. Usually, the right context is the context for which the invariant can be expressed in the simplest way and/or for which the invariant is simplest to check.

2.3.4 Using Association Classes

Association classes may also be used in OCL expressions, but some special rules apply. Association classes may not have a rolename; therefore, the name of the association class is used to refer to an instance of that class. The previous version of OCL also required that the class name be written starting with a lowercase letter. In version 2, the name used should be identical to the name of the association class. For instance, the following invariant uses the association class *Membership* to state that the service level of each membership must be a service level known to the loyalty program for which the invariant holds:

```
context LoyaltyProgram
inv knownServiceLevel: levels->
                            includesAll(Membership.currentLevel)
```

Using the association class as context, you may navigate to the instances of both classes at the end of the association to which the association class belongs, using their rolenames:

```
context Membership
inv correctCard: participants.cards->includes(self.card)
```

Because an association class is in fact a class itself, it can have ordinary associations with other classes. These may be referenced in the manner explained in Section 2.3.3. For example, the following defines a query operation to the association class *Membership* using the ordinary association between *Membership* and *ServiceLevel*:

```
context Membership
def : getCurrentLevelName() : String = currentLevel.name
```

2.3.5 Using Enumerations

In a UML model, enumeration types may be defined. An enumeration type may be used, for instance, as the type of an attribute of a class in a UML class model. The values of an enumeration type are indicated in an OCL expression by the name of the enumeration type, followed by two colons, followed by the value-name. An example can be found in the *CustomerCard* class, where the attribute *color* can have two values, either *silver* or *gold*. The following invariant states that the color of this card must match the service level of the membership:

```
context Membership
inv levelAndColor:
    currentLevel.name = 'Silver' implies card.color = Color::silver
    and
    currentLevel.name = 'Gold' implies card.color = Color::gold
```

2.4 WORKING WITH COLLECTIONS OF OBJECTS

Often, the multiplicity of an association is greater than 1, thereby linking one object to a collection of objects of the associated class. To deal with such a collection, OCL provides a wide range of collection operations, and distinguishes between different types of collections.

2.4.1 Using Collections Operations

Whenever navigation results in a collection of objects, you can use one of the *collection operations* to manipulate this collection. To indicate the use of one of the predefined collection operations, you place an arrow between the rolename and the operation. When you use an operation defined in the UML model, you use a dot.

The *size* Operation

For R&L, it would be reasonable to require that a loyalty program offers at least one service to its customers. Using the dot notation, you can navigate from the context of a loyalty program through its program partners to the services they deliver. This results in a collection of *Service* instances. With the arrow notation, you can apply the predefined operation *size*. The rule would be stated as follows:

```
context LoyaltyProgram
inv minServices: partners.deliveredServices->size() >= 1
```

The *select* Operation

Another invariant on the R&L model requires that the number of valid cards for every customer must be equal to the number of programs in which the customer participates. This constraint can be stated using the *select* operation on sets. The *select* operation takes an OCL expression as parameter. The result of *select* is a subset of the set on which it is applied, where the parameter expression is true for all elements of the resulting subset. In the following example, the result of *select* is a subset of *cards*, where the attribute *valid* is true:

```
context Customer
inv sizesAgree:
     programs->size() = cards->select( valid = true )->size()
```

The *forAll* and *isEmpty* Operations

Also relevant to the R&L model is a requirement that if none of the services offered in a *LoyaltyProgram* credits or debits the *LoyaltyAccount* instances, then these instances are useless and should not be present. We use the *forAll* operation on the collection of all services to state that all services comply with this condition. The *forAll* operation, like *select*, takes an expression as parameter. Its outcome is a boolean: true if the expression evaluates to true for all elements in the collection, and otherwise false. The following invariant states that when the *LoyaltyProgram* does not offer the possibility to earn or burn points, the members of the *LoyaltyProgram* do not have *LoyaltyAccounts*; that is, the collection of *LoyaltyAccounts* associated with the *Memberships* must be empty:

```
context LoyaltyProgram
inv noAccounts: partners.deliveredServices->forAll(
                  pointsEarned = 0 and pointsBurned = 0 )
                          implies Membership.account->isEmpty()
```

Note that defining a constraint for a class already implies that the condition holds for all instances of that class. There is no need to write the following:

```
context LoyaltyProgram
inv noAccounts: forAll( partners... )
```

In fact, this is an incorrect expression. The *forAll* operation is used when we already have a subset of all instances of a class, and we want to check on the elements of that subset. In the preceding example, all services delivered by the partners of a certain *LoyaltyProgram* are a subset of all instances of class *Service*. This subset is checked to include only those services for which *pointsEarned* and *pointsBurned* are equal to zero. (See Section 3.10.3 for more information on this topic.)

The preceding example also introduces two logical operations: *and* and *implies*. The *and* operation is the normal logical *and* operation on boolean values. The *implies* operation states that if the first part is true, then the second part must also be true; however, if the first part is not true, it does not matter whether the second part is true; the whole expression is true.

The *collect* Operation

A collection operation that is used very often is the *collect* operation. For instance, it is used when you want to get the set of all values for a certain attribute of all objects in a collection. In fact, many of the examples in this chapter use this operation, because the dot notation is an abbreviation for applying the *collect* operation. Take, for instance, the following expression in the context of *LoyaltyProgram*:

```
partners.numberOfCustomers
```

Another way to write it is

```
partners->collect( numberOfCustomers )
```

It means that for each element in the collection of partners of a loyalty program, the value of the attribute *numberOfCustomers* is added to a new collection, in this case, containing integer values.

The resulting collection is not a subset of the original collection. In fact, in most cases, the type of the elements in the resulting collection is different from the type of the elements in the manipulated collection. In this case, the collection *partners* contains elements of type *ProgramPartner*, whereas the collection resulting from applying the *collect* operation contains elements of type *Integer*.

The collect operation may be used not only to collect attribute values, but also to build a new collection from the objects held by association ends. The next expression, already used in this section, is an example of an implicit use of the *collect* operation on association ends:

```
partners.deliveredServices
```

Another way to write this expression is

```
partners->collect( deliveredServices )
```

For each element in the collection of partners of a loyalty program, the value of the association end *deliveredServices* is added to a new collection, in this case, containing references to instances of the class *Service*.

More Collection Operations

This section contains more collection operations (the complete list can be found in Chapter 9):

- *notEmpty*, which is true when the collection has at least one element
- *includes(object)*, which is true when *object* is an element of the collection
- *union(collection of objects)*, which results in a collection of objects that holds the elements in both sets

- *intersection(collection of objects)*, which results in a collection of objects that holds all elements that are in both collections

2.4.2 Sets, Bags, OrderedSets, and Sequences

When working with collections of objects, you should be aware of the difference between a *Set*, a *Bag,* an *OrderedSet,* and a *Sequence*. In a *Set*, each element may occur only once. In a *Bag*, elements may be present more than once. A *Sequence* is a bag in which the elements are ordered. An *OrderedSet* is a set in which the elements are ordered.

Navigations Resulting in Sets and Bags

To understand why these differences are important, take a look at the attribute *numberOfCustomers* of class *ProgramPartner*. We want to state that this attribute holds the number of customers who participate in one or more loyalty programs offered by this program partner. In OCL, this would be expressed as follows:

```
context ProgramPartner
inv nrOfParticipants:
        numberOfCustomers = programs.participants->size()
```

However, there is a problem with this expression. A customer can participate in more than one loyalty program. In other words, a reference to the same object of class *Customer* could be repeated in the collection *program.participants*. Therefore, this collection is a bag and not a set. In the preceding expression, these customers are counted twice, which is not what we intended.

In OCL, the rule is that when you navigate through more than one association with multiplicity greater than 1, you end up with a bag. That is, when you go from A to more than one B to more than one C, the result is a bag of Cs. When you navigate just one such association you get a set. There are standard operations that transform one of the types into any of the other types. Using one of these operations you can correct the previous invariant as follows:

```
context ProgramPartner
inv nrOfParticipants:
        numberOfCustomers = programs.participants->asSet()->size()
```

When you navigate an association with multiplicity greater than 1 on the target end, and from there navigate an association with multiplicity greater than 1 on the target end, you also end up with a bag. The expression *transactions.generatedBy* from the context of *CustomerCard* denotes a bag of instances of *Service*. Every service may be associated with more than one transaction, so when you take the services of a set of transactions, some services might be present more than once.

Navigations Resulting in OrderedSets and Sequences

When you navigate an association marked *{ordered}*, the resulting collection is of type *OrderedSet*; and following the rules explained above, when you navigate more than one association and one of them is marked *{ordered}*, you end up with a sequence. Several standard operations deal with the order of an ordered set or sequence: *first, last,* and *at(index).* The only ordered association in the R&L model lies between *LoyaltyProgram* and *ServiceLevel.* In the context of *LoyaltyProgram,* the expression *serviceLevel* results in an ordered set. We can state that the first element of this ordered set must be named *Silver* as follows:

```
context LoyaltyProgram
inv firstLevel: levels->first().name = 'Silver'
```

2.5 ADDING PRECONDITIONS AND POSTCONDITIONS

Preconditions and postconditions are constraints that specify the applicability and effect of an operation without stating an algorithm or implementation. Adding them to the model results in a more complete specification of the system.

2.5.1 Simple Preconditions and Postconditions

The context of preconditions and postconditions is specified by the name of the class that holds the operation and the operation signature (its name, parmeters, and return type). In the R&L example, the class *LoyaltyAccount* has an operation *isEmpty.*[1] When the number of points on the account is zero, the operation returns the value *true.* The postcondition states this more precisely; it tells us that the operation returns the outcome of the boolean expression *points = 0.* The return value of the operation is indicated by the keyword *result:*

```
context LoyaltyAccount::isEmpty(): Boolean
pre : -- none
post: result = (points = 0)
```

There is no precondition for this operation, so we include a comment, none, where the precondition should be placed, indicated by the double dash. Including a precondition, even if it is an empty one, is optional. Rather, it is a matter of style. We prefer to state even empty preconditions, because we think this is clearer. If, for instance, this example were part of a list of operations with their pre- and postconditions and the precondition for the *isEmpty* operation was the only one missing, the reader might misinterpret its meaning and think that the precondition was mistakenly forgotten.

---

[1] Note that this operation is different from the *isEmpty* operation defined on collections.

2.5.2 Previous Values in Postconditions

In a postcondition, the expression can refer to values at two moments in time:

- The value at the start of the operation
- The value upon completion of the operation

The normal value of an attribute, association end, or query operation in a post-condition is the value upon completion of the operation. To refer to the value of a property at the start of the operation, postfix the property name with the keyword *@pre*, as shown in the following example:

```
context Customer::birthdayHappens()
post: age = age@pre + 1
```

The term *age* refers to the value of the attribute after the execution of the operation. The term *age@pre* refers to the value of the attribute *age* before the execution of the operation.

When you need the pre-value of a query operation, the *@pre* is postfixed to the operation name, before the parameters, as shown in the next example:

```
context Service::upgradePointsEarned(amount: Integer)
post: calcPoints() = calcPoints@pre() + amount
```

The *@pre* postfix is allowed only in OCL expressions that are part of a postcondition.

2.5.3 Messaging in Postconditions

Another thing allowed only in postconditions is specifying that communication has taken place. This can be done using the *hasSent* ('^') operator. For example, you can specify the standard observer pattern:

```
context Subject::hasChanged()
post: observer^update(12, 14)
```

The *observer^update(12, 14)* results in true if an update message with arguments *12* and *14* was sent to the *observer* object during the execution of the operation *hasChanged()*. *update()* is either an operation defined in the class of *observer*, or a signal specified elsewhere in the UML model. The argument(s) of the message expression (*12* and *14* in this example) must conform to the parameters of the operation/signal definition.

2.6 TAKING INHERITANCE INTO ACCOUNT

The advantage of using inheritance is that an object using the superclass interface need not know about the subclasses. However, sometimes you explicitly want to mention the subclasses. In the R&L example, the program partners want to limit the number of bonus points they give away; they have set a maximum of 10,000 points to be earned using services of one partner. The following invariant sums all the points of all transactions for a partner. It does not specify our intent, however, because it does not differentiate between burning and earning transactions:

```
context ProgramPartner
inv totalPoints:
    deliveredServices.transactions.points->sum() < 10,000
```

To determine the subclass to which an element of this collection of transactions belongs, we use the standard operation *oclIsTypeOf*, which takes a class, datatype, component, or interface name as parameter. To retrieve from the collection all instances of this subclass, we use the *select* operation. We use the *collect* operation to retrieve from the collection of earning transactions a collection of points. These are the points that are summed by the operation *sum* and compared with the given maximum. Therefore, the correct invariant would be as follows:

```
context ProgramPartner
inv totalPointsEarning:
    deliveredServices.transactions
        ->select( oclIsTypeOf( Earning ) ).points->sum() < 10,000
```

2.7 COMMENTS

In any model, comments are necessary to facilitate human understanding. This holds for a UML/OCL model too. It is good practice to accompany every OCL expression with a comment. A line comment is indicated by two minus signs: --. After this marker, everything on the same line is considered to be comment. Comments that span more than one line can be enclosed between /* and */.

For example, the previous invariant could have been accompanied by the following comments:

```
/* the following invariant states that the maximum number of points
    that may be earned by all services of a program partner is equal
    to 10,000
*/
context ProgramPartner
inv totalPointsEarning:
    deliveredServices.transactions        -- all transactions
```

```
->select( oclIsTypeOf( Earning ) )  -- select earning ones
   .points->sum()                    -- sum all points
      < 10,000                       -- sum smaller than 10,000
```

2.8 LET EXPRESSIONS

Sometimes one writes large expressions in which a sub-expression is used more than once. The *let* expression enables you to define a variable that can be used instead of the sub-expression. The following example states that either the *validFrom* or the *goodThru* date of a customer card needs to be adjusted when the card is invalidated. An extra variable named *correctDate* is defined to indicate whether or not the current date is between the *validFrom* and *goodThru* dates:

```
context CustomerCard
inv: let correctDate : Boolean =
               self.validFrom.isBefore(Date::now) and
               self.goodThru.isAfter(Date::now)
     in
        if valid then
           correctDate = false
        else
           correctDate = true
        endif
```

A *let* expression may be included in any kind of OCL expression. The newly defined variable is known only within this specific expression.

2.9 SUMMARY

In this chapter, you have learned how to write OCL expressions by example. Of course, the description of OCL in this chapter is not complete, detailed, or precise. Part 2 of this book provides the complete specification of the OCL language. The following chapters in this part discuss how you can use OCL expressions for modeling.

Chapter 3

Building Models with OCL

This chapter shows how a UML model can be augmented by OCL expressions, resulting in a model that is rich enough to give to automated tools as input. All examples in this and the following chapters refer to the R&L system as depicted in Figure 2-1, unless stated otherwise.

3.1 WHAT IS A MODEL?

Before we discuss how to build a model, we need to understand what is meant by the word *model*. This term is used in many contexts and often has a different meaning. For instance, the R&L system depicted in the previous chapter is often called a *class model*. A statechart is sometimes called a *state model*. Are these models two separate, unrelated items, or should we consider them to be part of the same thing?

3.1.1 Definitions

In this book a model describes a system using a well-defined language. Therefore, the answer to the question above should be that both are views of the same model. Both class diagrams and the statecharts show items that describe the same system using the same language—namely, UML.

We use the word *model* to refer to a consistent, coherent set of model elements that have features and restrictions, where model elements are the compositional elements that may be used in artifacts written in UML and/or OCL. For example, classes are model elements, and so are states. Attributes and operations are features of classes, and derivation rules and invariants are restrictions on attributes and classes, respectively. Because most models are built using tools, we refer to the storage of all model elements as the *model repository*.

To indicate a certain view on the repository of model elements we use the word *diagram*. Using these definitions, the picture shown in Figure 2-1 is a *diagram* showing part of the R&L *model*. Model elements can be shown in one, in many, or in no diagrams. When an element is present in the model repository, it is part of the model. It need not be shown in any diagram. Nor is it necessary to show all of the features of a model element when one is present on a diagram. For instance, a class can be shown on two diagrams. On the first diagram, all attributes could be shown, but no operations. On the second diagram, all operations could be shown, but no attributes.

The definitions used in this book are summarized as follows:

> *A model is a consistent, coherent set of model elements that have features and restrictions.*

> *A model repository is the storage of all model elements in an automated tool.*

> *A diagram is a view of the model elements in a model.*

3.1.2 A Model Is a Consistent, Coherent Unit

Any model must be an integrated, consistent, and coherent unit. It must be crystal clear how entities shown in one diagram relate to entities in other visible parts of the model. In the previous example, it must be clear that in both class diagrams the same class is depicted. Likewise, it should be clear that the objects in an interaction diagram are instances of classes present in the model. These classes may be visible in one of the class diagrams. Another example of the relationship between model elements shown in different diagrams is the connection between a statechart, with all its states and transitions, and its owning class. This class must be present in the model, and may be shown in other diagrams. The attributes and operations of this class shown in the class diagram may also be shown in the statechart, e.g., in a guard to a transition.

OCL expressions are often not shown in any diagram, but they are still part of the model. They are present in the underlying repository. Automated tools will use the OCL expressions in a model in addition to the other information in the model. Therefore, we must establish how the UML diagrams and OCL expressions are connected. The relation between OCL expressions and entities shown on the diagrams must be clear. The link between an entity in a UML diagram and an OCL expression is called the *context definition* of an OCL expression.

3.1.3 The Context of an OCL Expression

The *context definition* of an OCL expression specifies the model entity for which the OCL expression is defined. Usually this is a class, interface, datatype, or component. For sake of convenience, we use the word *type* in the remainder of this book to indicate either class, interface, datatype, or component. In terms of the UML standard, this is called a *Classifier*, but we prefer to use the more intuitive word *type*.

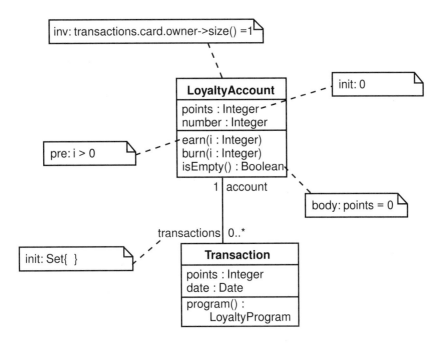

Figure 3-1 *OCL expressions and their context*

Sometimes the model entity is an operation, and rarely it is an instance. It is always a specific element of the model, usually defined in a UML diagram. This element is called the *context* of the expression.

Next to the context, it is important to know the *contextual type* of an expression. The contextual type is the type of the context, or of its container. It is important because OCL expressions are evaluated for a single object, which is always an instance of the contextual type. To distinguish between the context and the instance for which the expression is evaluated, the latter is called the *contextual instance*. Sometimes it is necessary to refer explicitly to the contextual instance. The keyword *self* is used for this purpose (see Section 6.1.2).

For example, the contextual type for all expressions in Figure 3-1 is the class *LoyaltyAccount*. The precondition (*pre: i>0*) has as context the operation *earn*. When it is evaluated, the contextual instance is the instance of *LoyaltyAccount* for which the operation has been called. The initial value (*init: 0*) has as context the attribute *points*. The contextual instance will be the instance of *LoyaltyAccount* that is newly created.

3.2 USE UML DIAGRAMS AS A BASE

When starting a new model, the first step is to build a number of diagrams. The most important diagram in the model is the class diagram. Because any model is structured around classes or components, this is where all information in the model is focused. The use of OCL strongly relies on the types (classes, datatypes, and so on) defined in a UML class diagram. This diagram should be built first. Other diagrams can be built according to need and taste.

The second step is to identify where the need for explicitly stating extra information lies. Following are some of the obvious situations that call for additional information:

- Elements might be underspecified; for instance, when an attribute has been defined as *derived*, but no derivation rule is given.
- Business rules must be incorporated into the model. This will result in a number of invariants, as shown in [Eriksson00].
- There is a need for a more precise definition of the interfaces in the system. This calls for the introduction of pre- and postconditions to operations.
- Finally, some aspects of the diagrams might be ambiguous without stating invariants.

The following sections describe a number of situations in which adding expressions to the diagrams is necessary to obtain a complete and unambiguous model.

3.3 COMPLETING CLASS DIAGRAMS

The model depicted in a class diagram can be augmented with extra information in numerous places. Most of the examples given in this section augment the class diagram for the R&L system shown in Figure 2-1 of Chapter 2.

3.3.1 Derivation Rules

Models often define derived attributes and associations. A derived element does not stand alone. The value of a derived element must always be determined from other (base) values in the model. Omitting the way to derive the element value results in an incomplete model. Using OCL, the derivation can be expressed in a derivation rule. In the following example, the value of a derived element *usedServices* is defined to be all services that have generated transactions on the account:

```
context LoyaltyAccount::usedServices : Set(Services)
derive: transactions.service->asSet()
```

Note that the question whether *usedServices* is an attribute or an association end should be answered from the UML diagram(s). In this case, it was not shown in the diagram in Chapter 2, so we cannot tell. Often, derived attributes are not shown in the diagrams at all, but are defined by an OCL attribute definition (see Section 3.9.1).

3.3.2 Initial Values

In the model information, the initial value of an attribute or association role can be specified by an OCL expression. In the following examples, the initial value for the attribute *points* is *0*, and for the association end *transactions*, it is an empty set:

```
context LoyaltyAccount::points : Integer
init: 0

context LoyaltyAccount::transactions : Set(Transaction)
init: Set{}
```

Note the difference between an initial value and a derivation rule. A derivation rule states an invariant: The derived element should always have the same value that the rule expresses. An initial value, however, must hold only at the moment when the contextual instance is created. After that moment, the attribute may have a different value at any point in time.

3.3.3 Body of Query Operations

The class diagram can introduce a number of query operations. Query operations are operations that have no side effects, i.e., do not change the state of any instance in the system. Execution of a query operation results in a value or set of values, without any alterations in the state of the system. Query operations can be introduced in the class diagram, but can only be fully defined by specifying the result of the operation. Using OCL, the result can be given in a single expression, called a *body expression*. In fact, OCL is a full query language, comparable to SQL, as shown in [Akehurs01]. The use of body expressions is an illustration thereof.

The next example states that the operation *getCustomerName* will always result in the name of the card owner associated with the loyalty account:

```
context LoyaltyAccount::getCustomerName() : String
body: Membership.card.owner.name
```

3.3.4 Invariants

Another way to augment a class diagram is by stating an invariant. The concept invariant is defined as follows:

> **An invariant is a boolean expression that states a condition that**

must always be met by all instances of the type for which it is defined.[1]

An invariant is described using an *boolean* expression that evaluates to true if the invariant is met. The invariant must be true upon completion of the constructor and completion of every public operation, but not necessarily during the execution of operations. Incorporating an invariant into a model means that any system made according to the model is faulty when the invariant is broken. How to react when an invariant is broken is explained in Section 4.6.2.

In the following example, all cards that generate transactions on the loyalty account must have the same owner:

```
context LoyaltyAccount
inv oneOwner: transactions.card.owner->asSet()->size() = 1
```

An invariant may be named, which can be useful for reference from an accompanying text. The preceding invariant is named *oneOwner*.

3.3.5 Preconditions and Postconditions

Preconditions and postconditions to operations are yet another way to complete the model depicted in a class diagram. Because pre- and postconditions do not specify how the body of an operation should be implemented, they are an effective way to precisely define the interfaces in the system. The concepts are defined as follows:

A precondition is a boolean expression that must be true at the moment that the operation starts its execution.

A postcondition is a boolean expression that must be true at the moment that the operation ends its execution.

Note that in contrast to invariants, which must always be true, pre- and postconditions need be true only at a certain point in time: before and after execution of an operation, respectively.

We can use OCL expressions to specify either the pre- and postconditions of operations on all UML types, or the pre- and postconditions of use cases. The first option is explained in this section, the second option is explained in Section 3.8.1. In the following example, a customer that is already known in the system, perhaps because it is already participating in another loyalty program, is enrolled in

---

[1] To be more precise, an invariant must be true in all consistent states of the system. While the system is, for instance, executing an operation, it is not in a consistent state, and the invariant need not be true. Of course, when the execution has finished, the invariant must again be true.

a loyalty program under the condition that its *name* attribute is not empty. The postcondition of the *enroll* operation ensures that the new customer is included in the list of customers belonging to the loyalty program:

```
context LoyaltyProgram::enroll(c : Customer)
pre : c.name <> ''
post: participants = participants@pre->including( c )
```

Note that a even a simple postcondition like *myVar = 10* does not specify any statement in the body of the operation. The variable *myVar* may become equal to *10* in numerous ways. Here are some example implementations in Java:

```
-- use another variable
otherVar = 10;
-- include other statements here
myVar = otherVar;

-- use a calculation
myVar = 100/10;

-- use another object
myVar = someElement;  -- where the value of someElement is 10
```

The principle behind the use of pre- and postconditions is often referred to as the *design by contract* principle. Design by contract can be used within the context of any object-oriented development method. The following paragraphs describe the principle and its advantages.

Design by Contract

The definition of *contract* in the design by contract principle is derived from the legal notion of a contract: a univocal, lawful agreement between two parties in which both parties accept obligations, and on which both parties can ground their rights. In object-oriented terms, a contract is a means to establish the responsibilities of an object clearly and unambiguously. An object is responsible for executing services (the obligations) if and only if certain stipulations (the rights) are fulfilled. A contract is an exact specification of the interface of an object. All objects that are willing to use the services offered are called *clients* or *consumers*. The object that is offering the services is called the *supplier*.

Although the notion of a contract is derived from law practice, it is not completely analogous when employed in object technology. A contract is offered by a supplier independently of the presence of any client. However, when a client uses the services offered in the contract, the client is bound by the conditions in the contract.

A contract describes the services that are provided by an object. For each service, it specifically describes two things:

- The conditions under which the service will be provided
- A specification of the result of the service that is provided, given that the conditions are fulfilled

An example of a contract can be found at most mailing boxes in the Netherlands:

> *A letter posted before 18:00 will be delivered on the next working day to any address in the Netherlands.*

A contract for an express service is another example:

> *For the price of two euros, a letter with a maximum weight of 80 grams will be delivered anywhere in the Netherlands within 4 hours after pickup.*

Table 3-1 shows the rights and obligations of both parties in the express delivery service example. Note that the rights of one party can be directly mapped to the obligations of the other party.

A contract can become much more complicated—for example, when it concerns the purchase of a house. The important point is that the rights and obligations in a contract are unambiguous. In software terms, we call this a *formal specification*. Both parties benefit from a clear contract:

- The supplier knows the exact conditions under which its services can be used. If the client does not live up to its obligations, the supplier is not responsible for the consequences. This means that the supplier can assume that the conditions are *always* met.
- The client knows the exact conditions under which it may or may not use the offered services. If the client takes care that the conditions are met, the correct execution of the service is guaranteed.

The interface that is offered by an object consists of a number of operations that can be performed by the object. For each operation, a contract can be envisioned. The rights of the object that offers the contract are specified by the preconditions. The obligations are specified by the postconditions.

If either party fails to meet the conditions in the contract, the contract is broken. When this happens, it is clear which party broke the contract: either the client did not meet the specified conditions or the supplier did not execute the service correctly. Failure of a precondition or postcondition—that is, either condition is not true when it should be—means that the contract is broken. In Eiffel, the only language that implements the design by contract principle, an exception is raised when a precondition or postcondition fails. In this way, the exception mechanism is an integral part of the design by contract principle.

Table 3-1 *Rights and obligations in a contract*

Party	Obligations	Rights
Customer	Pay two euros	Letter delivered within 4 hours
	Supply letter with weight less than 80 grams	
	Specify delivery address within Netherlands	
Express Service Company	Deliver letter within 4 hours	Delivery addresses are within the Netherlands
		Receive two euros
		All letters weigh less than 80 grams

3.3.6 Messaging in Postconditions

An aspect of postconditions that is very useful for defining interfaces is the fact that a postcondition may state that a certain operation has been called. For example, in the Eclipse framework, which is an open platform for tool integration built by an open community of tool providers (www.eclipse.org), every file is contained in a project. Several *builders*, which are responsible for keeping associated files up to date, can be linked with the project. An example of a builder is the Java compiler, which compiles a .java file into a .class file. When a file is saved, all builders are informed by calling their *incrementalBuild* operation. There is no need to uncover how the framework is taking care of this, but there is a need to inform Eclipse developers about this feature. A simple postcondition to the *save* operation of the class *File* will suffice:

```
context File::save()
post: self.project.builders->forAll( b : Builder |
                                     b^incrementalBuild() )
```

In general, when there is a need to specify dynamic aspects of a model element without revealing the actual implementation, the postcondition of the operations should contain message information. Note again that a postcondition does not specify any statement in the body of the operation. The message may have been sent in a number of different ways. The postcondition merely states that it is sent. Here are some possible example implementations in Java:

```
-- get all builders and loop over the collection
Builders[] builders = getProject().getBuilders();
for(int i=0; i<builders.size; i++) {
    builders[i].incrementalBuild();
}

-- let some other object take care of calling the builders
someObject.takeCareOfBuilders( getProject() );

-- let the project take care of calling the builders
getProject().callBuilders();
```

3.3.7 Cycles in Class Models

Many class models reflect *cycles* in the sense that you can start at an instance, navigate through various associations, and return to an instance of the same class. In the class diagram, this is shown as a cycle of classes and associations. Quite often, these cycles are the source of ambiguities.

The example used in Section 1.4.2, reprinted in Figure 3-2, shows a class diagram with a cycle. In this model, a *Person* owns a *House*, which is paid for by taking a *Mortgage*. The *Mortgage* takes as security the *House* that is owned by the *Person*. Although the model looks correct at first glance, it contains a flaw. Better stated, it is imprecise and can result in ambiguities. The model allows a person to have a mortgage that takes as security a house owned by another person. This is clearly not the intention of the model. We can easily state the necessary invariant with the following piece of OCL code:

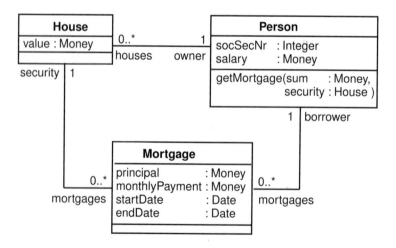

Figure 3-2 *A cycle in a class model*

```
context Person
inv: self.mortgages.security.owner
                        ->forAll(owner : Person | owner = self)
```

In general, cycles in a class model should be checked carefully, and any constraints on these cycles should be stated as invariants on one of the classes in the cycle. Especially when the multiplicities in a cycle are higher than one, you need to carefully write the invariant or invariants.

3.3.8 Defining Derived Classes

A view is a well-known concept in relational database systems. In a UML/OCL model, a similar concept exists. This concept is called a *derived class*. A derived class is a class whose features can be derived completely from already existing classes and other derived classes. The concept of derived classes has been introduced in [Blaha98], and formalized in [Balsters03].

For instance, in the R&L system, it might be useful to define a derived class that holds a transaction report for a customer, as shown in Figure 3-3. The attributes, association ends, and query operations of this class can be defined by the following expressions:

```
context TransactionReportLine::partnerName : String
derive: transaction.generatedBy.partner.name

context TransactionReportLine::serviceDesc : String
derive: transaction.generatedBy.description

context TransactionReportLine::points : Integer
derive: transaction.points

context TransactionReportLine::amount : Real
derive: transaction.amount

context TransactionReportLine::date : Date
derive: transaction.date
```

The class *TransactionReport* is not completely derived. Its *from* and *until* attributes are normal attributes without derivation rules. The other attributes can all be derived:

```
context TransactionReport::name : String
derive: card.owner.name

context TransactionReport::balance : Integer
derive: card.Membership.account.points
```

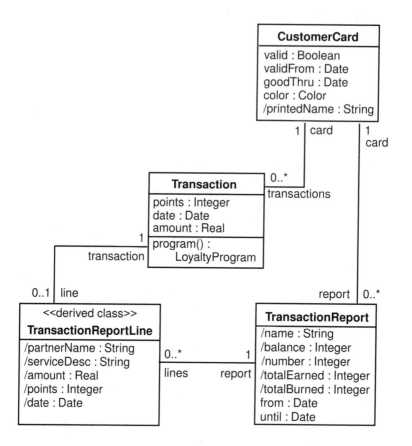

Figure 3-3 *A derived class*

```
context TransactionReport::number : Integer
derive: card.Membership.account.number

context TransactionReport::totalEarned : Integer
derive: lines.transaction->select( oclIsTypeOf( Earning ) )
            .points->sum()

context TransactionReport::totalBurned : Integer
derive: lines.transaction->select( oclIsTypeOf( Burning ) )
            .points->sum()
```

To complete the definition of this class, some invariants are needed. The *dates* invariant states that the transactions in this report should be transactions between the *from* and *until* dates. The *cycle* invariant states that the transactions in the lines of the report should indeed be transactions for this customer card:

```
context TransactionReport
inv dates: lines.date->forAll( d | d.isBefore( until ) and
                                    d.isAfter( from ) )

context TransactionReport
inv cycle: card.transactions->includesAll( lines.transaction )
```

3.3.9 Dynamic Multiplicity

Associations in a class diagram can sometimes be imprecise specifications of the system. This is the case when the multiplicity of the association is not fixed, but should be determined based on another value in the system. This is called *dynamic multiplicity*. An example of this has already been described in Section 1.4.1, where the multiplicity of the association between *Flight* and *Passenger* was indicated by the *numberOfSeats* on the *Airplane*.

3.3.10 Optional Multiplicity

An *optional multiplicity* of an association in a class diagram is often a partial specification of what is really intended. Sometimes the optionality is free; that is, in all circumstances there can be either one or no associated object. Quite often, an optional association is not really free. Whether an associated object can or must be present depends on the state of the objects involved. For example, in Figure 3-2, the optional association is not completely free. If a person has a mortgage, he or she must also own a house. This constraint can be specified by the following invariant:

```
context Person
inv optionality: mortgages->notEmpty() implies houses->notEmpty()
```

In general, when an optional multiplicity is present in the class diagram, you have to use OCL invariants to describe precisely the circumstances under which the optional association may be empty or not empty.

3.3.11 Or Constraints

The class diagram can contain an *or constraint* between two associations, as shown in Figure 3-4. This constraint means that only one of the potential associations can be instantiated at one time for any single object. This is shown as a dashed line connecting two or more associations (all of which must have at least one class in common), with the string *{or}* labeling the dashed line. The multiplicity of the associations must be optional; otherwise, they cannot be empty.

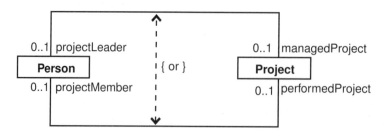

Figure 3-4 Or *constraint*

Note that the visual representation of an *or* constraint is ambiguous in certain situations. This is the case when two associations between the same two classes have multiplicity optional at both ends of both associations. The visual *or* constraint can now be read in two directions. In one direction, it can mean that one person has either a *managedProject* or a *performedProject*, but not both. In the other direction, it can mean that one project has either a *projectLeader* or a *projectMember*, but not both. Therefore, two different interpretations are possible.

Although the choice of interpretation may seem obvious in this case, you can imagine the consequences if someone makes the wrong interpretation. Specifying the visual *or* constraint as an OCL constraint resolves the ambiguity problem. When you intend the first interpretation, you should augment the diagram with the following invariant:

```
context Person
inv: managedProject->isEmpty() or performedProject->isEmpty()
```

The invariant stating the second interpretation is:

```
context Project
inv: projectLeader->isEmpty() or projectMember->isEmpty()
```

This example shows the importance of formal constraints and illustrates how they ensure that a model is unambiguous.

3.4 COMPLETING INTERACTION DIAGRAMS

OCL expressions may also be used to complete UML interaction diagrams. The example used in this section is the diagram shown in Figure 3-5. In the R&L system, new transactions are introduced through an operation of *LoyaltyProgram* called *addTransaction*. This operation takes five parameters:

1. The number of the account for which the transaction was performed, called *accNr* of type *Integer*
2. The name of the program partner that delivered the service for which the transaction was performed, called *pName* of type *String*
3. The identification of the service, called *servId* of type *Integer*
4. The amount paid for the service, called *amnt* of type *Real*
5. The date on which the transaction took place, called *d* of type *Date*

The *addTransaction* operation implements the following algorithm. First, the correct service is selected. This service calculates the points earned or burned by the transaction and creates a transaction object of the right type. This object is added to the service's association end *transactions*. Next, the correct account is selected. The newly created transaction is added to the transactions associated with this account, meanwhile adjusting the balance of the account. Finally, the correct card is selected and the new transaction is added to the transactions associated with this card. The algorithm is depicted in the sequence diagram.

As an elaborate example of an OCL postcondition, the *addTransaction* operation is also specified using a postcondition in the following OCL expression:

```
context LoyaltyProgram::addTransaction( accNr: Integer,
                                        pName: String,
                                        servId: Integer,
                                        amnt: Real,
                                        d: Date )
post: let acc : LoyaltyAccount =
            Membership.account->select( a | a.number = accNr ),
         newT : Transaction =
            partners-> select(p | p.name = pName)
               .deliveredServices
                  ->select(s | s.serviceNr = servId)
                     .transactions
                        ->select( date = d and amount = amnt ),
         card : CustomerCard =
            Membership->select( m |
                        m.account.number = accNr ).card
      in acc.points = acc.points@pre + newT.points          and
         newT.oclIsNew()                                     and
         amnt =  0 implies newT.oclIsTypeOf( Burning )       and
         amnt >  0 implies newT.oclIsTypeOf( Earning )       and
         acc.transactions - acc.transaction@pre = Set{ newT } and
         card.transactions - card.transaction@pre = Set{ newT }
```

3.4.1 Instances

In an interaction diagram, instances are shown. Because of our requirement that a model must be internally consistent, each instance shown must be of a type

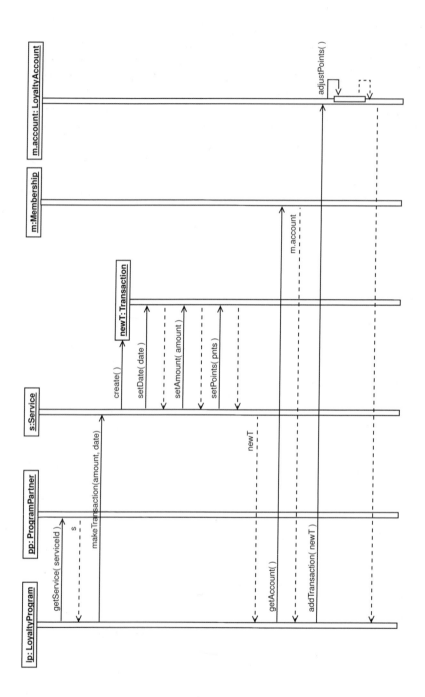

Figure 3-5 *OCL expressions in a sequence diagram*

declared in another diagram in the model. Usually, the other diagram is a class diagram. Furthermore, although no rules in UML state this explicitly, the target of a message in an interaction diagram must be known and visible to the source of the message. This can be indicated in the diagram using the name by which the target is known to the source. Formally, this has no meaning at all, but the human reader will probably find it useful. Another way to express this is to use your own names for the instances, and accompany the diagram with OCL expressions that state the relation between the instances.

In Figure 3-5, you can see that the instance of *LoyaltyAccount* is named *m.account*, where *m* references the *Membership* instance in the diagram. To state the relationship between the other instances in the diagram, the following expressions can be used:

```
lp.partners->includes(pp) and pp.name = pName
pp.deliveredServices->includes( s ) and s.serviceNr = servId
lp.Membership->includes( m ) and m.account.number = accNr
```

3.4.2 Conditions

A part of the interactions in a sequence or collaboration diagram can have an attached condition that specifies in what circumstances the part is executed. This condition can be written as an OCL expression.

Because an interaction diagram is an instance diagram, the OCL expression is written in the context of an instance, not a type. This is a rare case; therefore, extra attention has to be paid to determine the contextual type and the contextual instance. The contextual instance is the instance on whose lifeline the condition is written, and the contextual type is the type of this instance.

An example can be found in Figure 3-6, which extends the sequence diagram in Figure 3-5. The service object *s* creates a transaction of the right type, depending on the *amnt* parameter of the *addTransactions* operation. The conditions are written

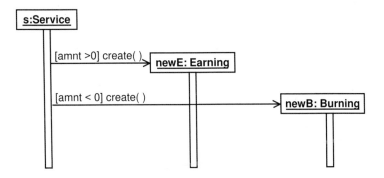

Figure 3-6 *Extended interaction diagram*

as valid OCL expressions, given the fact that the diagram specifies an operation, and therefore the parameters of the operation can be used.

3.4.3 Actual Parameter Values

A message in an interaction diagram is not equivalent to the specification or definition of an operation or signal, but instead represents an operation call or the sending of a signal. Both operations and signals can take parameters. The parameters of a message are not the formal parameters but actual values. For instance, when an operation is defined, its name and the name and type of every parameter is given, as in *setValue(i: Integer)*. When an operation is called, its formal parameters are substituted by actual values, as in *setValue(235)*.

To specify the actual value of a parameter to a message, you may use an OCL expression. In the example shown in Figure 3-5, the value to be substituted for the parameters of operation *addT* is provided by *newT*, a reference to the newly created transaction instance.

Note that a message to an object in an interaction diagram must conform to an operation in the type of the target object, or to a signal that has been elsewhere defined. Conformance here means that the name of the operation is the same, and the parameters in the message are of the types indicated for the parameters of the operation. Likewise, the result message in an interaction diagram (a dotted arrow in the sequence diagram, or an assignment in the collaboration diagram) must be of the type indicated as the result type of the called operation.

3.5 COMPLETING STATECHARTS

In UML statecharts, OCL expressions may be used in a number of ways. In all cases, the contextual type is the class to which the statechart belongs, and the contextual instance is the instance for which a transition in the statechart fires.

The example in this section is a simple process-control system in a factory that produces bottles with certain liquid contents. The classes used are depicted in Figure 3-7. The process is as follows: A line object takes a new bottle object from its stock, and triggers a filler object to fill this bottle. The bottle monitors its contents and messages the filler when it is full. The filler then triggers the line to move the bottle to the capper, which caps the bottle. Figure 3-8 contains the statechart for class *Filler*, and Figure 3-9 contains the statechart for class *Bottle*.

3.5.1 Guards

OCL expressions can be used to express *guards* in statecharts. A guard is a condition on a transition in a statechart. A guard is often included in the statechart diagram itself. In that case, it is written between square brackets ([and

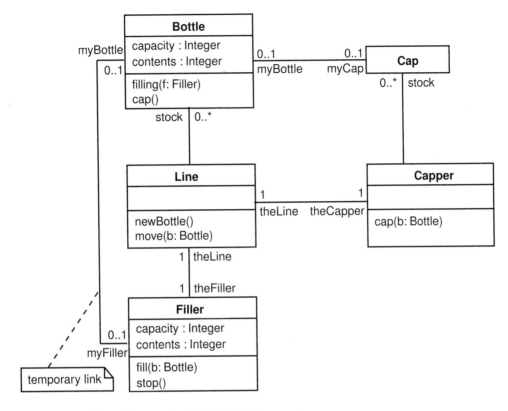

Figure 3-7 *Class diagram for the bottle-filling system*

]) after the event that triggers the transition. In Figure 3-8, you can find a guard on the transition from the state *stopped* to the state *filling*. In this case, the *Filler* object will change state only if it contains enough liquid.

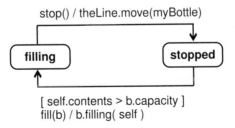

Figure 3-8 Filler *statechart*

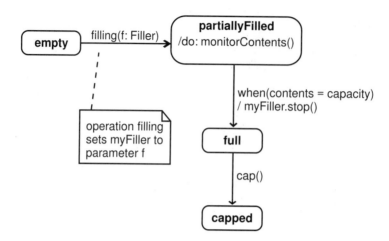

Figure 3-9 Bottle *statechart with change event*

3.5.2 Target of Actions

An action in a statechart represents either an operation call or the sending of an event. Actions may be coupled to transitions or states in a statechart. When coupled to a transition, the action is executed if and when the transaction fires, and is targeted at a specific object or set of objects. When coupled to a state, the action is executed when the state is entered; when a state is left; or when an indicated event occurs. In the last case, usually the target is the *self* object.

To identify the target of an action, whether coupled to a transition or a state, an OCL expression can be used. For example, the action *theLine.move(b)* in Figure 3-8 has as its target the *Line* object linked to the contextual instance of *Filler,* and the action *myFiller.stop()* in Figure 3-9 has as its target the *Filler* object linked to the contextual instance of *Bottle.*

3.5.3 Actual Parameter Values

Because actions represent operation calls or the sending of events, and both can have parameters, actions in statecharts can have parameters. Like the parameters to messages in an interaction diagram, these are actual values, not the formal parameters of the corresponding operation or sent event. The value of such a parameter can be specified using an OCL expression, in which case the context of the expression is the transition or state to which the action is coupled. In Figure 3-8, both actions have an actual value as parameter.

3.5.4 Change Events

A *change event* is an event that is generated when one or more attributes or associations change value. The event occurs whenever the value indicated by the expression changes from false to true. A change event is denoted by the keyword *when*, parameterized with an OCL expression. For example, in the state transition diagram of the *Bottle* class in Figure 3-9, a change event is attached to the transition from state *partiallyFilled* to state *full*. The transition takes place as soon as the condition *contents = capacity* becomes true. No externally generated event is needed.

Note that a change event is different from a guard condition. A guard condition is evaluated once when its event fires. If the guard is false, the transition does not occur, and when no other transition for the same event is specified, the event is lost. When a change event occurs, a guard can still block any transition that would otherwise be triggered by that change.

3.5.5 Restrictions on States

Usually, there are restrictions on values of links and attributes when an object is in a certain state. These should be specified explicitly. For instance, for the class *Bottle*, the following invariants should hold:

```
context Bottle
inv: (self.oclInState(capped) or self.oclInState(full))
                                    implies contents = capacity
inv: (self.oclInState(empty) implies contents = 0
inv: self.oclInState(capped) implies myCap->notEmpty()
inv: self.oclInState(partiallyFilled) implies myFiller->notEmpty()
```

3.6 COMPLETING ACTIVITY DIAGRAMS

To complete the specification of activity diagrams, OCL expressions can be used in the same ways as in interaction diagrams:

- To indicate instances
- To specify conditions
- To specify actual parameter values

For activity diagrams, an OCL expression can be used to indicate the instance that is executing an activity. The contextual instance for all expressions in the diagram is the instance that executes (or controls) the overall activity that contains this diagram as a specification of its internal implementation.

Activity diagrams are also used to specify the flow of a complete system or business. In that case no object executes the overall activity. (One might argue that the system or company executes the overall activity.) Therefore, the keyword *self* cannot be used. See Section 3.8 for a further discussion of the implications of this case.

Figure 3-10 shows the specification of the operation *addService(s:Service, p:ProgramPartner)* of class *LoyaltyProgram*. This diagram contains examples of all possible uses of OCL. The first activity (from the top) takes one actual parameter: *s.level*. This the *ServiceLevel level* from the *Service s*. Both the first and second activities from the top are executed by the contextual instance indicated by the keyword *self*, whereas the middle activity is executed by the program partner instance that is the parameter *p*, and the last one is executed by parameter *s*. The conditions shown at both choices are simple OCL expressions.

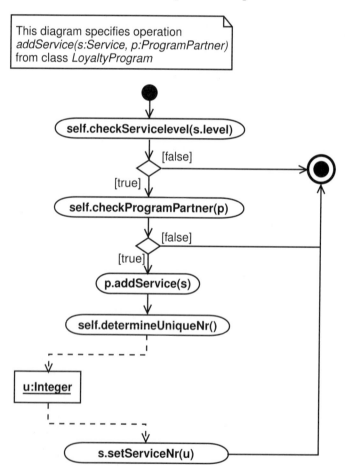

Figure 3-10 *Activity diagram specifying operation* addService

3.7 COMPLETING COMPONENT DIAGRAMS

There is not much use for OCL expressions in component or deployment diagrams. It is only when elements usually depicted in a class diagram are present in a component or deployment diagram that OCL expressions can be used.

For instance, when a component diagram contains explicit specifications of interfaces, the operations in the interfaces can be specified using pre- and postconditions. An example of this situation can be found in Figure 3-11, which is taken from the UML specification itself.

Besides interfaces, classes may be shown in a component diagram. For these, the same options discussed in Section 3.3 hold.

3.8 COMPLETING USE CASES

In UML use cases, pre- and postconditions may be used. These may also be written using OCL. Because use cases are an informal way of stating requirements, and OCL is a formal language, some adjustments need to be made when the pre- and postconditions of use cases are to be defined using OCL expressions.

3.8.1 Preconditions and Postconditions

Although use cases can be considered to be operations defined on the complete system, we cannot identify the complete system as a type, because it is not a class, an interface, a datatype, or a component. Therefore, the pre- and postconditions of a use case have no contextual type or contextual instance. As a consequence, the keyword *self* cannot be used.

In addition, it is not clear which model elements may be referenced in the expression. Normally, all elements held by the contextual type may be used. Here, there is no contextual type. Therefore, the model elements that may be used must be explicitly stated. This can be done by formalizing the types mentioned in the use case, e.g., *Customer* and *Order*, in an accompanying class diagram; and adding to the use case template a section called (for instance) *concerns*, with a list of variable declarations, e.g., *newCustomer : Customer, newOrder : Order.*

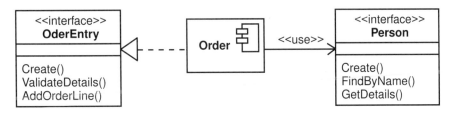

Figure 3-11 *Component diagram*

Yet another consequence is that we cannot write a context definition, as there is no contextual type to be referenced. This is not a problem. The OCL expressions may be directly included in the use case at the position indicated by the use case template.

The following example illustrates a use case for the R&L system. It describes how customer cards are upgraded and how invalid cards are removed from the system. Because not all information about the attributes and operations in the system could be included in Figure 2-1, the *CustomerCard* class—with all attributes used in the following use case—is reprinted in Figure 3-12.

Use case title: Check customer cards for loyalty program
Summary: On a regular basis the cards of all participants in a loyalty program are checked. Those that have been invalidated are removed, and those that have been used often are upgraded to the next service level.
Primary actor: user
Uses: - the class diagrams for the Royal & Loyal system as shown in Figure 2-1 and Figure 3-12
  - *lp* of type *LoyaltyProgram*, which is the loyalty program for which the cards are checked
  - *upgradeLimit* of type *Integer*, which indicates how many points must have been earned before a card is upgraded
  - *fromDate* of type *Date*, which gives the date from which to calculate points to see if an upgrade is required
Precondition: none
Main success scenario:
1. The actor starts the use case and gives the *upgradeLimit*. This value must be larger than 0.
2. The system selects all cards that have been invalidated or have a goodThru date that lies before today, and shows them to the user.
3. The actor checks the invalid cards, and marks any card that must not be removed by giving a new *goodThru* date.

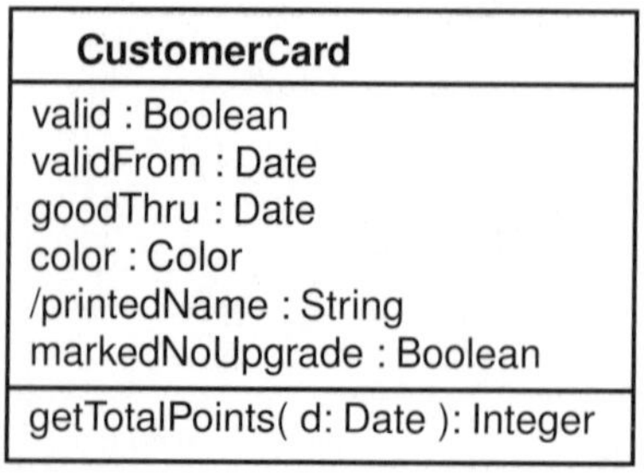

CustomerCard
valid : Boolean
validFrom : Date
goodThru : Date
color : Color
/printedName : String
markedNoUpgrade : Boolean
getTotalPoints(d: Date): Integer

Figure 3-12 *Class* CustomerCard, *with all its attributes and operations*

4. The system removes all invalid cards, except the ones that have received a new *goodThru* date.
5. The actor gives the *fromDate*. This date must be before today.
6. The system calculates for all remaining cards the number of points earned in the period starting with *fromDate* until today, and shows the cards for which this number is higher than the *upgradeLimit*.
7. The actor checks the cards to be upgraded, and marks any card that must not be upgraded.
8. The system upgrades the selected cards.
Extensions:
   -- indicate what is to be done when the *upgradeLimit* and *fromDate*
   -- do not uphold their conditions
Postcondition:
-- all *goodThru* dates are in the future

```
lp.participants.cards.goodThru->forAll( d | d.isAfter( Date::now )
and
-- all cards that have earned enough points and have not been marked
-- otherwise are upgraded
let upgradedCards : Set( CustomerCard ) =
        lp.participants.cards->select( c |
            c.getTotalPoints( fromDate ) >= upgradeLimit
            and c.markedNoUpgrade = false )
in
    upgradedCards->forAll( c |
        lp.levels->indexOf( c.Membership.currentLevel ) =
        lp.levels->indexOf( c.Membership.currentLevel@pre ) + 1
```

3.9 MODELING STYLES

Apart from mending apparent flaws in the model, OCL expressions can also be used to express the same information in a different manner. There are various styles of modeling. This section explains some of the different modeling styles.

3.9.1 Definitions of Attributes or Operations

Attributes or operations may be defined in the class diagram by adding them to a type, but they may also be defined by an OCL expression. In that case, the new attribute or operation need not be shown in the diagram. In the following example, two attributes, *wellUsedCards* and *loyalToCompanies*, and one operation, *cardsForProgram*, are defined:

```
context Customer
def: wellUsedCards : Set( CustomerCard )
        = cards->select( transactions.points->sum() > 10,000 )
def: loyalToCompanies : Bag( ProgramPartner )
```

```
          = programs.partners
def: cardsForProgram(p: LoyaltyProgram) : Set(Cards)
          = p.Membership.card
```

The expression following the equal sign in an attribute definition indicates how the value of the attribute must be calculated. It is a derivation rule (see Section 3.3.1). For example, the newly defined attribute *loyalToCompanies* is always equal to the collection of program partners associated with the programs, in which the customer is enrolled. The attribute *wellUsedCards* is always equal to the set of cards for which the total of points earned with the transactions carried out with that card is larger than 10,000.

The expression following the equal sign in an operation definition states the result of the operation. It is a body expression (see Section 3.3.3). Note that operations defined by an OCL expression are query operations. They cannot have side effects. In the preceding example, the operation *cardsForProgram* will always result in the set of cards issued for the loyalty program *p* provided as a parameter to the operation.

3.9.2 The Subset Constraint

A class diagram may contain *subset constraints*, as shown in Figure 3-13. This constraint means that the set of links for one association is a subset of the set of links for the other association. In Figure 3-13, *flightAttendants* is a subset of *crew*. The singleton set *pilot* is also a subset of *crew*.

By showing all subset constraints in the diagram, it may become cluttered and difficult to read. In that case, you may choose to specify the subset constraints using OCL expressions. The two subset constraints shown in Figure 3-13 are identical to the following invariants on *Flight* and *Person*:

```
context Flight
inv: self.crew->includes(self.pilot)
inv: self.crew->includesAll(self.flightAttendants)
```

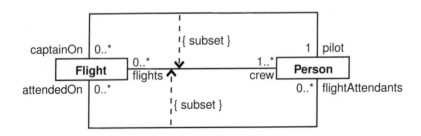

Figure 3-13 *A subset constraint*

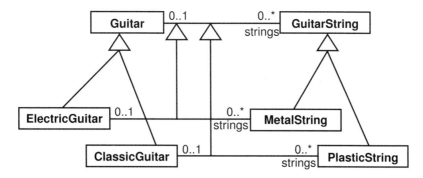

Figure 3-14 *Model with specializations*

```
context Person
inv: self.flights->includes(self.captainOn)
inv: self.flights->includesAll(self.attendedOn)
```

3.9.3 Adding Inheritance Versus Invariants

During modeling, we often encounter situations in which we add detail to the class model to specify the real-world situation precisely. For example, suppose we have a simple class diagram of a guitar, in which a guitar has a number of guitar strings. Furthermore, there are two types of guitars: electric and classic. We also have two types of guitar strings. Each guitar type has its own kind of guitar strings.

The association between *Guitar* and *GuitarString* specifies that a *Guitar* has *GuitarString*s. The association between *ClassicGuitar* and *PlasticString* is a redefinition of the same association, which constrains a *ClassicGuitar* to have *PlasticString*s only. The generalization between the associations shows that the lower association is a specialization of the upper, more general association. The association between *ElectricGuitar* and *MetalString* is also a redefinition of the top association. This situation is depicted in Figure 3-14.

As you can see, the model becomes comparatively complex. It can be simplified using invariants. The two specializations of the upper association can be captured in two invariants on the two types of guitars, as depicted in the class model shown in Figure 3-15. The visual class model becomes more readable, while the level of detail is retained. The invariants are as follows:

```
context ClassicGuitar
inv strings1: strings->forAll(s | s.oclIsTypeOf(PlasticString) )

context ElectricGuitar
inv strings2: strings->forAll(s | s.oclIsTypeOf(MetalString) )
```

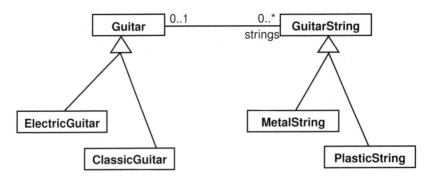

Figure 3-15 *Model without specialized associations*

The preceding model can be simplified even more by removing the subclasses of *Guitar*, *GuitarString*, or both. If the main reason for having the subclasses is to distinguish between different kinds of strings for different guitars, this simplification makes sense. Depending on the situation, this simplification may result in either Figure 3-16 or Figure 3-17.

Here are the invariants for the class model shown in Figure 3-16:

```
context ClassicGuitar
inv strings3: strings->forAll(type = StringType::plastic)

context ElectricGuitar
inv strings4: strings->forAll(type = StringType::metal )
```

Here are the invariants for the class model shown in Figure 3-17:

```
context Guitar
inv strings5: type = GuitarType::classic implies
                 strings->forAll(type = StringType::plastic)
```

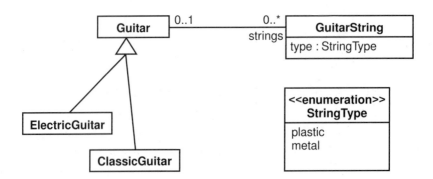

Figure 3-16 *Model without some of the subclasses*

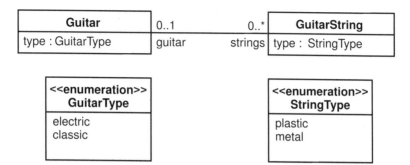

Figure 3-17 *Class model without subclasses*

```
context Guitar
inv strings6: type = GuitarType::electric implies
                  strings->forAll(type = StringType::metal )
```

The deciding factor in the trade-off that must be made in these circumstances is which solution will be best in your situation. Figure 3-17 keeps the model simple, because there is no need for subclasses. If no attributes or behaviors are specific to the subclasses, this is a good solution. In Figure 3-16, we have a more elaborate model that is suitable when there *are* attributes or operations specific to the different subclasses. In Figure 3-14, we have an elaborate model with probably too much detail. This option is desirable only if you want to show all details in the visual diagram. In general, showing your model in graphical or visual form is best for giving a good overview, whereas a textual form is good for adding detail. The art is finding the right balance, and that depends on both the intended use of the model and the intended audience.

3.10 TIPS AND HINTS

This section provides some tips and hints about how to write meaningful OCL expressions.

3.10.1 Avoid Complex Navigation Expressions

Using OCL, we can write long and complex expressions that navigate through the complete object model. We could write all invariants on a class model starting from only one context, but that does not mean that it is good practice to do so.

Any navigation that traverses the whole class model creates a coupling between the objects involved. An essential aspect of object orientation is encapsulation. Using a long navigation makes details of distant objects known to the object from which we started the navigation. If possible, we would like to limit the object's knowledge to only its direct surroundings, which are the properties of the type, as described in Section 8.1.

Another argument against complex navigation expressions is that writing, reading, and understanding invariants becomes very difficult. It is hard to find the appropriate invariants for a specific class, and maintaining the invariants when the model changes becomes a nightmare.

Consider the following expression, which specifies that a *Membership* does not have a *loyaltyAccount* if you cannot earn points in the program:

```
context Membership
inv noEarnings: programs.partners.deliveredServices->
    forAll(pointsEarned = 0) implies account->isEmpty()
```

Instead of navigating such a long way, we might want to split this constraint. We define a new attribute *isSaving* for *LoyaltyProgram*. This attribute is true if points can be earned in the program:

```
context LoyaltyProgram
def: isSaving : Boolean =
        partners.deliveredServices->forAll(pointsEarned = 0)
```

The invariant for *Membership* can use the new attribute, rather than navigate through the model. The new invariant looks much simpler:

```
context Membership
inv noEarnings: programs.isSaving implies account->isEmpty()
```

3.10.2 Choose Context Wisely

By definition, invariants apply to a type, so it is important to attach an invariant to the right type. There are no strict rules that can be applied in all circumstances, but the following guidelines will help:

- If the invariant restricts the value of an attribute of one class, the class containing the attribute is a clear candidate.
- If the invariant restricts the value of attributes of more than one class, the classes containing any of the attributes are candidates.
- If a class can be appointed the responsibility for maintaining the constraint, that class should be the context. (This guideline uses the notion of responsibility-driven design [Wirfs-Brock90].)
- Any invariant should navigate through the smallest possible number of associations.

Sometimes it is a good exercise to describe the same invariant using different classes as context. The constraint that is the easiest to read and write is the best one to use. Attaching an invariant to the wrong context makes it more difficult to specify and more difficult to maintain.

As an example, let's write an invariant in several ways. The invariant written for the diagram shown in Figure 3-18 states the following: two persons who are married to each other are not allowed to work at the same company. This can be expressed as follows, taking *Person* as the contextual object:

```
context Person
inv: wife.employers->intersection(self.employers)->isEmpty()
     and
     husband.employers->intersection(self.employers)->isEmpty()
```

This constraint states that there is no company in the set of employers of the wife or husband of the person that is also in the set of employers of the person. The constraint can also be written in the context of *Company*, which creates a simpler expression:

```
context Company
inv: employees.wife->intersection(self.employees)->isEmpty()
```

In this example, the object responsible for maintaining the requirement will probably be the *Company*. Therefore, *Company* is the best candidate context for attaching the invariant.

3.10.3 Avoid *allInstances*

The *allInstances* operation is a predefined operation on any modeling element that results in the set of all instances of the modeling element and all its subtypes in the system. An invariant that is attached to a class always applies to all instances of the class. Therefore, you can often use a simple expression as invariant instead of using the *allInstances* predefined operation. For example, the following two invariants on class *Person* (which is not depicted) are equivalent, but the first is preferred:

```
context Person
inv: parents->size <= 2
```

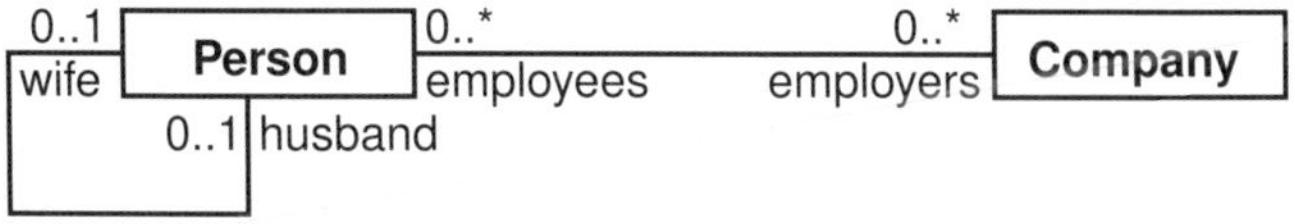

Figure 3-18 Persons *working for* Companies

```
context Person
inv: Person.allInstances->forAll(p | p.parents->size <= 2)
```

The use of *allInstances* is discouraged, because it makes the invariant more complex. As you can see from the example, it hides the actual invariant. Another, more important, reason is that in most systems, apart from database systems, it is difficult to find all instances of a class. Unless an explicit tracking device keeps a record of all instances of a certain class as they are created and deleted, there is no way to find them. Thus, there is no way to implement the invariant using a programming language equivalent of the *allInstances* operation.

In database systems, the *allInstances* operation can be used for types that represent a database table. In that case, the operation will result in the set of objects representing all records in the table.

3.10.4 Split *and* Constraints

Constraints are used during modeling, and they should be as easy to read and write as possible. People tend to write long constraints. For example, all invariants on a class can be expressed in one large invariant, or all preconditions on an operation can be written as one constraint. In general, it is much better to split a complicated constraint into several separate constraints. It is possible to split an invariant at most *and* operations. For example, you can write an invariant for *ProgramPartner* as follows:

```
context LoyaltyProgram
inv: partners.deliveredServices->forAll(pointsEarned = 0)
     and
     Membership.card->forAll(goodThru = Date.fromYMD(2000,1,1))
     and
     participants->forAll(age() > 55)
```

This invariant is completely valid and useful, but you can rewrite it as three separate invariants, making it easier to read:

```
context LoyaltyProgram
inv: partners.deliveredServices->forAll(pointsEarned = 0)
inv: Membership.card->forAll(goodThru = Date::fromYMD(2000,1,1))
inv: participants->forAll(age() > 55)
```

The advantages of spliting invariants are considerable:

- Each invariant becomes less complex and therefore easier to read and write.
- When you are determining whether an invariant is appropriate, the discussion can focus precisely on the invariant concerned, instead of on the complex invariant as a whole.

- When you are checking and finding broken constraints in an implementation, it is easier to determine the part that is broken. In general, the simpler the invariant, the more localized the problem.
- The same arguments hold for pre- and postconditions. When a precondition is broken during execution, the problem can be pinpointed much more effectively when you are using small, separate constraints.
- Maintaining simpler invariants is easier. If you need to change one condition, then you need change only one small invariant.

3.10.5 Use the *collect* Shorthand

The shorthand for the *collect* operation on collections, as defined in Section 9.3.11, has been developed to streamline the process of reading navigations through the class model. You can read from left to right without being distracted by the *collect* keyword. We recommend that you use this shorthand whenever possible, as shown in the following:

```
context Person
inv: self.parents.brothers.children->notEmpty()
```

This is much easier to read than

```
context Person
inv: self.parents->collect(brothers)
                    ->collect(children)->notEmpty()
```

Both invariants are identical, but the first one is easier to understand.

3.10.6 Always Name Association Ends

In case of multiple associations between the same classes, naming the association ends is mandatory. However, even when it is not mandatory, naming association ends is good practice. An exception can be made in the case of directed or non-navigable associations, for which only the ends that are navigable need to be named.

The name of an association end, like the name of an attribute, indicates the purpose of that element for the object holding the association. Furthermore, naming association ends is helpful during the implementation, because the best name for the attribute (or class member) that represents the association is already determined.

3.11 SUMMARY

In this chapter you have learned how a model can benefit from OCL expressions. For every UML diagram, we have indicated where OCL expressions can be added.

The class diagram may benefit from OCL expressions stating derivation rules, initial values, body of query operations, invariants, and preconditions and post-conditions. OCL expressions can also be helpful in specifying cycles, defining derived classes, and specifying dynamic and optional multiplicity.

In component or deployment diagrams, OCL expressions can be used to specify explicitly mentioned interfaces and classes.

The interaction diagram and activity diagram can be improved by specifying instances and actual parameter values, and by stating conditions.

The statechart may be augmented with guards, explicit targets of actions, and actual parameter values. Change events and restrictions on states can also be expressed using OCL.

In a use case, the pre- and postconditions can be written using OCL.

Finally, we examined different modeling styles, and learned some useful tips for building models.

Chapter 4

Implementing OCL

This chapter describes how OCL expressions can be implemented in code. Although the Java language is used in the examples, the principles explained can be applied using any object-oriented programming language as target language. Even a non-object-oriented language could be used, but the process would be more cumbersome.

The process of mapping OCL expressions to code can be perfomed manually or by automated tools. Several available tools can translate OCL to code. Because the tool market is rapidly changing, we do not provide a list of tools in this book; it would be outdated quickly. Instead, on the Web site http://www.klasse.nl/ocl/ you can find an up-to-date list of tools that are currently available.

This chapter does not systematically treat the mapping of all OCL constructs. A systematic treatment would basically be a specification of an OCL compiler which would be very space consuming and to some extent boring to read. Instead, this chapter describes the main challenges and solutions of implementing OCL.

4.1 IMPLEMENTATION PROCESS

UML and OCL are not programming languages but specification languages, i.e., a UML/OCL model specifies how a system should be structured and what it should do, not how it should be implemented. The models are usually not directly compiled and executed. There is, however, a strong connection between the implementation of a system and the model that specifies it. Certainly within the context of MDA, the connection between the model and its implementation(s) is getting stronger and should be stated clearly.

In this chapter, we explain how to generate Java code from a combined UML/OCL model. Our focus, of course, is on how to build code from OCL expressions. However, as the UML class diagram must be built before writing OCL expressions, the first step in implementing the model is to define the implementation of the model elements defined in the class diagram(s).

In the next step, the OCL expressions can be translated. Their translation uses the implementation of the model elements. For instance, when an attribute has been implemented by a private class member with a *get* and a *set* operation for that member, the implementation of an OCL expression referencing this attribute must use the corresponding *get* operation.

Furthermore, the code fragments translated from the OCL expressions must be used according to their role in the model (invariant, attribute definition, derivation rule, and so on). The code fragments should be placed in the implementation in such a way that they fulfil their purpose.

The order of steps described in the implementation process is as follows:

1. Define the implementation of the UML model elements.
2. Define the implementation of the OCL standard library.
3. Define the implementation of the OCL expressions.
4. Place the code fragments implementing the OCL expressions correctly in the code for the model elements.
5. For invariants, and pre- and postconditions, decide when to check them, and what to do when the check fails.

The second step needs to be done only once, and can easily be done outside a specific project context. The results will be re-usable over all projects.

Because OCL is a declarative language, it specifies *what* should be calculated, but not *how* to calculate the value of an expression. Therefore, the translation from OCL to code that we show in this chapter includes a number of implementation options. These are by no means the only ones or the best ones. In other circumstances, you might need to make other choices.

The rest of this chapter is structured according to the preceding steps.

4.2 IMPLEMENTING UML MODEL ELEMENTS

Implementing UML model elements means implementing user-defined classes, datatypes, and so on. About the implementation of these types we can be short: Use the manner of implementation you prefer. The only thing you need to take care with, is maintaining the connection with the implementation of the OCL expressions in step 3. For instance, if an association is implemented by two class members, each placed in one of the classes at both sides of the association, the implementation of an OCL expression that refers to the association must refer to the right class member.

In this chapter, we assume that the following rules are used to implement user-defined types. Our R&L example has no components or datatypes; therefore, no rule for implementing them is given. In practice, they follow rules similar to the ones given here:

Classes   Every user-defined class is implemented in one Java class.

Operations Every operation on the class in the model is implemented by one operation in the Java class.

Attributes Every attribute (private, protected, or public) of the class in the model is implemented by a private class member and a *get* and *set* operation in the Java class. The visibility of the operations is identical to the visibility of the corresponding attribute in the model. If the attribute is marked *read-only*, the *set* operation is omitted. The *get* operation always has the form *AttributeType getAttributename()*. The *set* operation always has the form *void setAttributename (AttributeType newValue)*.

Associations Every association end of the class in the model is implemented by a private class member and a *get* and *set* operation in the Java class. The name of the class member is the name of the role at that end. Again, the visibility of the operations is identical to the visibility of the corresponding association end in the model.

If the multiplicity of the association end is greater than one, the type of the class member is either the Java implementation of the OCL *Set* or *OrderedSet*, depending on the ordering of the association. In this case, an *add* and *remove* operation are added to the implementation of the contextual type, which can add or remove an element from the class member.

States Every state defined in a statechart for a class is implemented by a boolean class member. Additional invariants are added to ensure that an instance of the class can be in only one state at a time. When a state has substates, the invariants are adjusted to accommodate them. The class member representing the parent state and one of the class members representing the substates may be true at the same time.

Events Every event defined in a statechart for that class is implemented by an operation with the same name. This operation implements the reaction of the instance on the event. The reaction must take into account the state of the instance, any conditions on transitions that are triggered by the event, and any actions connected to the transitions or to the begin and end state of the transitions. In other words, we assume that a statechart has a protocol interpretation. Pre- and postconditions of the event operations are inferred from the statechart in terms of the state members of the class.

Enumerations Every enumeration type is implemented by one Java class, holding static public class members for each value.

Interfaces Every interface is implemented by one Java interface.

As an example, the implementation of the *CustomerCard* class from the R&L system is provided in Appendix D.

4.3 IMPLEMENTING THE OCL STANDARD LIBRARY

In this section, we implement the OCL Standard Library in two different parts. First, we define the implementation of the basic types, such as *Integer* and *String*. Second, we show how the OCL collection types can be implemented.

4.3.1 OCL Basic Types

The mapping of the predefined basic types and model types is, although not straightforward, relatively easy because its problems are well known. The predefined basic OCL types, and their literals and operations, should be mapped to basic types in the target language. For instance, the Java programming language offers the types *float* and *double*, whereas OCL has only one *Real* type. You need to choose how the *Real* type is to be implemented by Java code, either by *float* or by *double*. Because the basic types of most programming languages are very similar, this mapping will not constitute many problems. Table 4-1 shows the mapping that we use.

After defining this mapping, we need to map all operations from these OCL types to operations in Java. Because Java does not provide counterparts for all operations defined on the OCL basic types, we need to define a special library that will hold the OCL operations not provided directly in Java. This can be done by defining a library class in which each required operation is defined as a static Java method.

The following code shows an example of a library class containing operations that are not available as operations in the standard Java types:

```
class OclIntegerOperations {

    static public int max(int i1, int i2) {
```

Table 4-1 *Mapping of basic types from OCL to Java*

OCL Type	Java Type
Integer	int
Real	float
String	String
Boolean	boolean
OclType	Class
OclAny	Object

```
    if( i1 > i2 ) { return i1; } else { return i2; }
  }

  static public int min(int i1, int i2) {
    if( i1 < i2 ) { return i1; } else { return i2; }
  }

}
```

Using these definitions, we can translate the following OCL expressions:

```
i1.max (i2)
i1.min (i2)
```

The corresponding Java code would be as follows:

```
OclIntegerOperations.max(i1, i2)
OclIntegerOperations.min(i1, i2)
```

In fact, the Java library includes a class, *java.lang.Math*, that defines the *min* and *max* operations exactly as described above. Therefore, in this case, we could have used the *Math* class instead.

Mapping the operations defined on every OCL type, such as *oclIsTypeOf* and *oclIsKindOf*, is slightly more complicated. Usually, these operations can be mapped on similar constructs defined on the root class in the target language. For instance, in Java, the keyword *instanceof* can be used to implement *oclIsKindOf*, and the *getClass* method of the root class *Object* can be used to implement *oclIsTypeOf*.

For example, we might define our own class *OclAny* as follows:

```
class OclAny {

  static oclIsTypeOf(Object o, String classname) {
    return o.getClass().getname().equals(classname);
  }

}
```

Using this class, we can translate the following OCL expression:

```
o.oclIsTypeOf(Type)
```

The corresponding Java code would be

```
OclAny.oclIsTypeOf(o, "Type");
```

Another option is to define your own class for each basic type in OCL. The preceding static operations then become straightforward nonstatic operations of such a class. This solution works along the lines of the Java *Integer* class, which represents a built-in Java *int* as a real object. The static operations *min* and *max* can then be implemented as follows:

```
class OclInteger extends java.lang.Integer {

    public OclInteger(int value) {
        super(value);
    }

    public OclInteger max(OclInteger i2) {
        if( this.intValue() > i2.intValue() ) {
            return this;
        } else {
            return i2;
        }
    }

    public OclInteger min(OclInteger i2) {
        if( this.intValue() < i2.intValue() ) {
            return this;
        } else {
            return i2;
        }
    }

}
```

Using these definitions, we can translate the following OCL expression:

```
i1.max (i2)
i1.min (i2)
```

The corresponding Java code would be

```
i1.max(i2)
i1.min(i2)
```

The disadvantage is that this new class must be used as the type for every integer in the Java code, instead of the built-in Java classes. Many Java libraries and APIs expect standard Java types as their parameters. Wherever this is the case, we have to use the *intValue()* operation, defined in *java.lang.Integer*, to get an *int* out of our

OclInteger. In addition, we need to transform each *int* that we receive—e.g., as parameter—to a new *OclInteger* object. Therefore, this solution is highly unpractical, and we have chosen not to use this approach.

4.3.2 OCL Tuples

Because tuples are types that are defined on the fly, there are no explicit type definitions for tuples in the model. Nor does the Java language need explicit tuple types. You may easily use any implementation of the *Map* interface from java.util.

As an alternative, you can choose to define a separate Java class for each tuple type. This is safer, because it ensures proper type checking in the Java code. Additionally, this option is much faster at runtime, because fetching a field from a tuple can be done directly. Using the *Map* implementation, a string-based lookup needs to be performed. A disadvantage is the extra coding that needs to be added.

4.3.3 OCL Collection Types

OCL collection types should be mapped to the collections in one of the libraries of the target language; when the target language does not provide collections, we have to build our own. Java provides a large number of different collection types—for instance, *Set*, *Tree,* and *List*. Choose one for each OCL collection type. It is usually best to stick to this choice for every mapping that needs to be made. That is, always use the same Java class for implementing an OCL *Set*, another for implementing an OCL *Bag*, and so on. Because there are no direct counterparts for *Bag* and *OrderedSet*, we need to choose a closely matching type to represent these. Table 4-2 shows a possible mapping.

OCL collections have a large number of predefined operations. These operations come in two flavors—the ones that loop over the collection (see Section 9.3), e.g., *select*, *exists*, and *collect*, and the ones that don't, e.g., *union* and *size*. Any operation in the first category is called an *iterator*, or *collection iterator*. Operations in the latter category are simple collection operations. Both categories need to be implemented differently.

Table 4-2 *Mapping of collection types from OCL to Java*

OCL Collection Type	Java Type	Concrete Type
Set	Set	HashSet
Sequence	List	ArrayList
Bag	List	ArrayList
OrderedSet	List	ArrayList

Simple collection operations

Simple collection operations can be mapped to operations on the target language collection types. When they are not present, you have two options. The first option is to define your own classes to represent the OCL collection types by inheriting from a standard collection type. The remaining OCL operations that cannot be mapped directly can be implemented on these classes.

The disadvantage of this approach was already explained in Section 4.3.1. These user-defined classes need to be used as the type for every collection object in the Java code, because the OCL expressions use collection-typed fields in the Java code. For this reason, we have not chosen this option.

The approach we have taken in Appendix D is to use the Java collection classes from the standard Java libraries, adding the additional operations required for implementing OCL as static Java methods in a separate library class. In this case, you can use ordinary Java collections anywhere, and you refer to the special static methods only when you evaluate an OCL expression. A simple example of a class containing the static methods is shown in the following code:

```
public class OclCollectionOperations {

  public static boolean notEmpty(Collection c) {
    (c == null) || (!c.isEmpty() == 0);
  }

}
```

Note that *Collection* in the preceding code refers to the Java Collection interface (java.util.Collection). Using this class, the following OCL expression can be translated:

```
someCollection->notEmpty()
```

The corresponding Java code would be as follows:

```
OclCollectionOperations.notEmpty(someCollection);
```

Note that the (Java) type of *someCollection* must implement the Java Collection interface.

Collection Iterators

The collection iterators are usually more difficult to implement. Fitting counterparts for the operations that loop over collections cannot be found easily. Preferably, the OCL standard library would be implemented by a library in the target programming language. Unfortunately, this is not possible for most languages, because the implementations of many standard operations that loop over a collection should take a piece of code as a parameter. Only a few programming languages support this. For instance, it would be very straightforward if you could translate the next OCL expression into one single Java expression:

```
context Customer
inv: cards->select( valid = true )->size() > 1
```

The Java expression would need to take the code that represents the *valid = true* part as a parameter to the select operation:

```
// the following is incorrect Java
getCards().select( {valid == true} ).size() > 1
```

In Java, the preceding code is illegal, because you cannot use a block of Java code as a parameter to a method. The (Java) definition of the *select* method would have to look like the following:

```
// the following is an incorrect Java implementation
// of operation 'select' on class Set
Set select( JavaExpression exp ) {
   // body of operation
   // exp should repeatedly be executed here
   // for each element in the collection
}
```

When you work in Smalltalk or any other language that supports expressions as first-class objects, you should take advantage of this aspect of the language to define your own classes that implement the OCL standard library. If you work with a programmming language that does not support expressions as first-class objects, every use of a collection iterator requires a specially designed code fragment. In this chapter, we use the Java language; thus, we are limited in the design choices we can make.

Because all collection iterators loop over a collection, the specially designed code fragment uses the looping mechanisms of the target language to implement the loop. In Java, looping is usually implemented using the *Iterator* class. For instance, the following OCL expression, in which *source* is a *Set*, is implemented by a rather complex piece of Java code, using a Java *Iterator* instance on *source*:

```
source->select(a=true)
```

The implementing Java code is as follows:

```
Iterator it = source.iterator();
Set result = new HashSet();
while( it.hasNext() ){
```

```
        ElementType elem = (ElementType) it.next();
        if ( elem.a == true ){
            result.add(elem);
        }
    }
    return result;
```

In only two places in this code fragment can the OCL expression be recognized. These are shown in boldface. The first is a reference to the collection *source*; the second is the test *a == true* from the body of the select operation. Furthermore, the code fragment needs to explicitly mention the type of elements in the collection *source*. For example, in the preceding code fragment, the type is called *Element-Type*.

When the test of the *select* iterator, or any of the other iterators, is more complex, it is more difficult to recognize it in the implementing code. For instance, to get all program partners for which all services have no points to be earned, from the context of a *LoyaltyProgram*, we can use the following OCL query:

```
self.partners->select(deliveredServices->forAll(pointsEarned =0))
```

This results in the following piece of Java code. The lines are numbered to facilitate further explanation:

```
1.   Iterator it = this.getPartners().iterator();
2.   Set selectResult = new HashSet();
3.   while( it.hasNext() ){
4.       ProgramPartner p = (ProgramPartner) it.next();
5.       Iterator services = p.getDeliveredServices().iterator();
6.       boolean forAllresult = true;
7.       while( services.hasNext() ){
8.           Service s = (Service) services.next();
9.           forAllResult = forAllResult && (s.getPointsEarned() == 0);
10.      }
11.      if ( forAllResult ){
12.          selectResult.add(p);
13.      }
14.  }
15.  return result;
```

Parts of the original OCL expression can be recognized in the code; for every navigation, the corresponding *get* operation is called. These calls are printed in boldface in lines 1, 5, and 9. The rest of the code needs some unraveling. Lines 1 and 2 prepare the loop that implements the *select* operation: a Java iterator and the result set are initialized. Lines 3 through 14 represent the *select* loop, which embeds the *forall* loop. The *forall* loop is initialized in lines 5 and 6, and executed in lines 8 through 10. The test *pointsEarned = 0* can be found in line 9, also printed in boldface.

The following code illustrates a template for the implementation of *collect* in Java. This piece of code implements the general expression

```
source->collect(attr)
```

We assume that *source* is a *Set*, and *attr* is of type *AttrType*:

```
1.   Iterator it = source.iterator();
2.   Set result = new HashSet();
3.   while( it.hasNext() ){
4.      ElementType elem = (ElementType) it.next();
5.      AttrType attr = (AttrType) elem.getAttr();
6.      if ( !(attr instanceof ClassImplementingOclCollection) ) {
7.         result.add( attr );
8.      } else {
9.         // repeat this template in case attr is a collection
10.     }
11.  }
12. return result;
```

Note that because the *collect* iterator flattens collections (see Section 9.3.10), i.e., the result is never a collection of collections but always a collection of object references or values, we have to determine whether *attr* itself is a collection. This is implemented in line 6, using the type *ClassImplementingOclCollection*. If *attr* is a collection, line 9 needs to be expanded using the same *collect* template. The template will need to be recursively repeated until elements that are not collections themselves are reached. In order to generate this code, we need to do a careful analysis to determine whether we are dealing with collections of collections, and to which depth the collections are nested.

Another approach to this problem is to implement a separate *flatten* operation in the previously mentioned *OclCollectionOperations* class. We can then remove the test in line 6. After the *while* loop, we flatten the entire result collection:

```
1.   Iterator it = source.iterator();
2.   Set result = new HashSet();
3.   while( it.hasNext() ){
4.      ElementType elem = (ElementType) it.next();
5.      AttrType attr = (AttrType) elem.getAttr();
6.      result.add( attr );
7.   }
8.   result = OclCollectionOperations.flatten(result);
9.   return result;
```

Each iterator in OCL (*select, exists, forAll, collect,* and so on) will have its own template, which needs to be filled with the details in the OCL expression to be implemented. These templates can be optimized. For example, the *forAll* template, as used in one of the preceding examples, can be written in such a way that the loop stops as soon as the result is found to be false. Of course, this means that the Java code will become even lengthier and more difficult to read; therefore, optimization was not used in the example.

The examples in this section show that expressions dealing with collections in OCL are more comprehensive than the corresponding Java code. As a result, the OCL expressions are easier to write; more important, they are much easier to read and understand than the Java code. This is desirable because the OCL expressions are part of the software's specification, whereas the Java code is part of the implementation. Specifications should be easier to read and write. When a specification is easy to read and write, and meanwhile it is as precise and unambiguous as the implementing code, it serves as good input to the MDA process.

4.4 IMPLEMENTING OCL EXPRESSIONS

Once you have decided how to implement the model elements and the OCL standard library, you are ready for step 3, as described in Section 4.1. You now need to consider the implementation of the OCL expressions themselves. Although this looks rather straightforward, the following sections describe some issues that need careful attention.

4.4.1 Evaluation Order

Evaluation order is not (and does not need to be) defined in OCL; it is perfectly legal to write a constraint and have part of that constraint *undefined* (see Section 10.6). For example, consider the following invariant in the R&L model:

```
context Membership
inv: account.points >= 0 or account->isEmpty()
```

Intuitively, this might be translated into the following fragment of Java code:

```
(this.getAccount().getPoints() >= 0)
||
(this.getAccount() == null)
```

If there is no *account*, the sub-expression *account.points >= 0* evaluates to *undefined* in OCL, and the sub-expression *account->isEmpty()* evaluates to true. In OCL, the result of the full invariant is true and well defined. However, if you generate code directly from the invariant as described, and the execution order is left to right, the *this.getAccount().getPoints()* code will try to reference a nonexisting object (*account*). Usually, this leads to a runtime error (e.g., *java.lang.nullPointerException*), so care must be taken to avoid such situations.

In the Java code, you need to add a test to determine whether certain objects exist. In the preceding example, you should write the following:

```
( (this.getAccount() == null)
||
(this.getAccount().getPoints() >= 0)
```

In this piece of Java code, the *nullPointerException* can never occur.

4.4.2 No Side Effects

An OCL expression should always be treated as an atomic expression. No changes of value of any object in the system can take place during the evaluation of the expression. In purely sequential applications, this might not be a problem, but in a parallel, multi-user environment, it must be addressed. The values referenced in a single OCL expression should be visible and reachable from the thread that executes the implementation of the expression.

4.4.3 Getting Attribute and AssociationEnd Values

The code for getting an attribute value depends on the way in which attributes from the UML model are mapped to Java. In the mapping described in Section 4.2, the value of an attribute named *attribute* can be obtained through the operation *getAttribute()*. Therefore, any attribute reference in OCL needs to be mapped to the corresponding *get* operation. For instance, the OCL expression

```
self.attribute
```

is transformed into the following Java code:

```
this.getAttribute();
```

The Java code to get the value of an association end depends on the mapping of the UML association in the same way. The solution in Section 4.2 maps an association end to a Java private attribute with a corresponding *get* operation. This means that the OCL navigation of an association will become an operation call in Java. For instance, the OCL expression

```
self.associationEnd
```

is transformed into the following Java code:

```
this.getAssociationEnd();
```

If another implementation for attributes or associations is chosen, then the implementation of the OCL expressions should follow this.

4.4.4 Let Expressions

In OCL *let* expressions, local variables are defined. Likewise, a *let* expression can be implemented by defining a local variable. In the next example, the operation *selectPopularPartners* selects program partners that have generated numerous large transactions after the given date. Its postcondition is stated in terms of the transactions generated by these partners:

```
context LoyaltyProgram::selectPopularPartners( d: Date )
                                          : Set(ProgramPartner)
post: let popularTrans : Set(Transaction) =
         result.deliveredServices.transactions->asSet()
      in
         popularTrans->forAll( date.isAfter(d) ) and
         popularTrans->select( amount > 500.00 )->size() > 20000
```

This expression can be implemented using a local variable in the separate operation that implements the postcondition (see Section 4.5.2). Note, of course, that the scope of the local variable must be at least equal to the scope of the OCL expression in which the *let* variable is used.

4.4.5 Treating Instances as Collections

In OCL, an object can be treated as a collection, as in *instance->size()*. In programming languages, this is not very common. The simplest way to translate such an expression into Java is to introduce a temporary collection that holds the instance as the only element. For instance, the following OCL expression from the context of *Membership* uses a *LoyaltyAccount* object as collection:

```
account->size()
```

It can be implemented by the following Java code. Again, the parts of the OCL expression that can be recognized are printed in boldface:

```
Set coll = new HashSet();
if( account != null ) coll.add( account );
return coll.size();
```

The check for *account != null* is necessary to ensure that we never put the null value in the created set. If we did, the result of the Java code would be incorrect.

Another option to implement this specific OCL expression is to determine whether the object reference is equal to null, as shown in the following code:

```
if( account != null ) return 1;
else return 0;
```

This option results in simpler Java code, but is less general, because it implements the *size* operation in a specific manner.

4.5 MERGING CODE FRAGMENTS

The code fragments that implement OCL expressions must be merged with the code that implements the part of the system specified by the UML diagrams. Each OCL expression should be used according to its purpose in the model. For most expressions, this is simple. The code for an attribute definition clearly belongs in the code for the class that is mentioned in the context definition. The code for the initial value of an attribute must be placed where the attribute is created or initialized. If the body of a query operation is given as an OCL expression, the implementing code for that expression will become the body of the operation. For other expressions, such as derivation rules, invariants, and pre- and postconditions, there are more options, which makes the merging of the code fragment for the OCL expression into the code for the contextual type slightly more complicated.

4.5.1 Derivation Rules

Derivation rules can be implemented in two different ways. The method chosen depends on the complexity and usage of the derivation rule.

The most straightforward approach is to implement an attribute with a derivation rule as a query operation, where the derivation rule serves as the body of the operation. Each time the attribute value is requested, the derivation will be calculated. The example in Appendix D takes this approach.

If the evaluation of the rule is expensive and the attribute is frequently used, the aforementioned strategy might not be optimal. As an alternative, the value of the attribute can be stored as an attribute. However, the object that contains the attribute needs to be notified in case any change occurs in the objects upon which the derivation depends. The listener or observer pattern can be used to set up such a notification mechanism. Each time the value of the attribute is requested, you can determine whether it needs to be recalculated.

In any case, a derived attribute should never have a public *set* operation, because no other object should be able to change its value.

4.5.2 Invariants

The best way to implement an invariant is to write a separate operation with a boolean result that implements the check. This operation can be called whenever it is appropriate to check the invariant. It is convenient to include one operation in a class that calls all separate operations that implement invariants, because often all invariants need to be checked at the same time.

The most important issue is to determine when to call these operations. This is treated in Sections 4.6.1 and 4.6.2. Note that model elements referred to in the invariant should be passed as parameters to the operation that implements the invariant.

4.5.3 Preconditions and Postconditions

Pre- and postconditions can best be implemented in the operation for which they are defined. Some languages provide an assert mechanism that can be used. For example, the following operation specification can be easily implemented using the Java *assert*:

```
context LoyaltyProgram::enroll(c : Customer)
pre : not participants->includes(c)
post: participants = participants@pre->including(c)
```

Assuming the operations *includes* and *including* are provided for *participants*, the resulting code in the class *LoyaltyProgram* is as follows:

```
Void enroll(Customer c) {
    assert( ! participants.contains(c) );
    old_participants = new ArrayList(participants);
    // ...
    // < body of operation >
    // ...
    assert( participants = old_participants.add(c) );
}
```

When the postcondition uses precondition time values (see Section 10.1.1), the implementing code should hold those values in a temporary variable. In the preceding example, *old_participants* is used to hold the value of the *participants* association end. Note that the old value must be a true copy or clone, not a copy of the reference, because the referenced value will change during the operation.

Usually, checking postconditions explicitly is not done. It does not add much value to the implementation. Postconditions are more a means to improve and clarify specifications. Implementing preconditions, conversely, is very useful. The source of a runtime error that causes a precondition to fail is much easier to find than an arbitrary runtime error.

4.5.4 Guards and Change Events in Statecharts

The implementation of guards and change events in a statechart depends on how the statechart and its transitions are implemented. When the transitions are implemented by operations, i.e., the event at the transition is actually an operation call to which the object responds, the guard should be considered part of the precondition of the operation. In that case, the start state should also be considered part of the precondition. The end state is considered part of the postcondition. Implementing them follows the rules for implementing pre- and postconditions.

For example, the statechart in Figure 3-8, reprinted in Figure 4-1, may be implemented by the following operations in class *Filler*:

```
void stop() {
    if (!pre_stop()) {
        system.out.println("precondition failed in stop");
    }
    theLine.move(getMyBottle());
    state = stopped;
}

void fill(Bottle b) {
    if (!pre_fill(b)) {
        system.out.println("precondition failed in fill(b)");
    }
    b.filling( this );
    myBottle = b;
    state = filling;
}
```

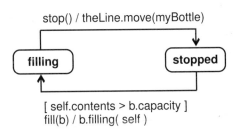

stop() / theLine.move(myBottle)

filling   stopped

[self.contents > b.capacity]
fill(b) / b.filling(self)

Figure 4-1 Filler *statechart, reprinted from Figure 3-8*

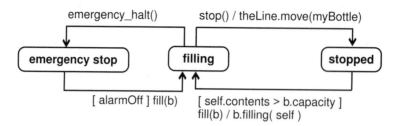

Figure 4-2 *Extended* Filler *statechart*

```
boolean pre_stop() {
    return state == filling;
}

boolean pre_fill(Bottle b) {
    return state == stopped &&
            this.getContents() > b.getCapacity();
}
```

When the same event occurs as a trigger for more than one transition, the situation is more complex. In this case, we must take into account all possible situations at precondition time; therefore, we must implement the precondition to be the or-ed combination of all possibilities. For example, the statechart shown in Figure 4-2, an extention of the previous example, contains the event *fill(b)* twice. In this case, the precondition to the operation *fill* may be implemented by the following code:

```
boolean pre_fill(Bottle b) {
    return (state == stopped &&
            this.getContents() > b.getCapacity())
            ||
            (state == emergencystop && this.alarmOff );
}
```

When a statechart is implemented by a statemachine, using the real-time interpretation of statecharts, the OCL expressions need to be implemented in a different manner. Guards should be implemented as conditions on the execution of the actions and state change specified by the transition. The following pseudocode gives an example. Note that a correct implementation of the OCL expressions depends completely on the way the statemachine is implemented.

```
while( true ) {
    e = get_eventId();
    if (e != null) {
        switch (e) {
            1: if ( guard_on_1 ) {
                // execute actions and state change
            }
            2: if ( guard_on_2 ) {
                // execute actions and state change
            }
            // etc.
        }
    }
}
```

4.5.5 Code for Interaction Diagrams

Because interaction diagrams are instance diagrams, they are not complete specifications, but examples of interactions between instances. Interaction diagrams
can be used to provide a skeleton of the code of the operations that are visible in
the diagrams, but they cannot be used to generate the complete Java code. The
OCL expressions used for conditions, target objects of messages, and parameters
of messages all become part of the operation skeletons. For example, based on the
diagrams in Figures 3-5 and 3-6, the following operation should be added to the
code for class *Service*:

```
Transaction makeTransaction(float amnt, Date d) {
    Transaction newT;
    if (amnt > 0 ) {
        newT = new Earning();
    } else if ( amnt == 0 ) {
        newT = new Burning();
    }
    newT.setDate(d);
    newT.setAmount(amount);
    // calculate pnt
    newT.setPoints(pnt);
    return newT;
}
```

It may very well be that this code should be completed with extra (hidden) functionality. All we know from the diagrams is that the preceding calls should be
present somewhere in the operation body and that the order of calls should be as
stated.

4.6 CONSIDERATIONS FOR CONSTRAINTS

When implementing constraints, you must decide when to check them and what to do when a constraint fails.

4.6.1 When to Check Constraints

Invariants are defined as being true at any moment in time, but in a runtime system they cannot be checked continuously. One solution to this problem is to check the invariants on an object immediately after any value in the object has changed. For example, when the value of an attribute changes, all invariants that refer to the attribute would be checked. Of course, this might include invariants on objects other than the object that is being changed, and checking could prove to be expensive.

How often and when to check an invariant depends on how serious the error could be. Invariants on objects in a customer relationship management system might be checked once a week or whenever the object is used, whereas the aforementioned expensive solution might be the right one to check objects in a crucial process-control system. You need to find a solution that balances complete checking with runtime efficiency in a way that is right for your situation.

Preconditions should be checked each time the operation is called. However, depending on the complexity of the precondition and the performance requirements, the cost of this technique might be prohibitive. In circumstances where the software is used as a component, offering services to other unknown components, it is wise to always check preconditions—to avoid incorrect use and potential disaster as a result of it. If the software is used as part of a closed, well-defined system, precondition checking should be turned on during testing, but might be turned off during production.

Postconditions are naturally checked at the end of the execution of an operation. Practice has shown that precondition checking is much more important than postcondition checking. Therefore, if the possibility for checking is limited, preconditions are the best candidates to check.

This leads to another question: whether you want constraints—invariants as well as pre- and postconditions—to be checked during deployment. Practice has shown that during system development, checking is very useful. When the system is deployed, checking might take too much processor time, making the system slower than necessary. In that case, an assert mechanism that can be switched on and off is very useful. For instance, in systems built with the Eiffel language, preconditions are often checked during development, testing, and debugging, but not checked (or only partially checked) when the application is operational. The Java language also includes an assertion mechanism, although it can only be controlled in a rather coarse-grained fashion.

Whether constraints need to be checked during deployment depends on the type of system you are dealing with. In an average database system, it is not unusual to have corrupted data. Unless the percentage of corrupted data grows too large, it is no problem. In such a case, the database administrator might run a check of all invariants every couple of weeks, and clean the database based on the results. If the correctness of the data is (much) more important, the invariants could be checked upon every change of value. A broken constraint can lead to a rollback of the transaction in which the failure occurs.

The same argument holds for precondition checking. Only when the precondition represents a vital aspect of the system does it need to be checked each time the operation is called. In other circumstances, far less checking is necessary.

4.6.2 What to Do When a Constraint Fails

Another issue is how one should react when a constraint is broken; in other words, what action has to be taken when the restrictions laid on the objects are no longer met? Consider three different approaches to broken constraints.

The simplest one is to print an error message each time a constraint is broken. Although this might seem a very low-level approach, it still is a very effective one, especially when constraints are checked only during development of the system, and not during deployment. Constraint checking during development is a way to continuously test the software.

Some people argue that breaking a constraint should throw some kind of exception, or at least that such behavior should be an option. In Eiffel, assertions are used both as a debugging tool and as an exception facility; this means that when the assertion (or, in our terms, the constraint) is broken, an exception is thrown. In Java, which incorporates the concept of assertions, this approach is used as well.

Others argue that the breaking of a constraint is a trigger for an operation to be executed. For instance, in Soma, the analysis and design method defined by Ian Graham [Graham95], rules can be triggers to actions that the system must undertake. An example of a possible action in a transaction environment is to roll back the transaction.

4.7 SUMMARY

This chapter has discussed how OCL expressions can be implemented. The translation of the expressions to programming code must be done according to the following steps:

1. Define the implementation of the UML model elements. Use any manner you like, provided that the choices made can be used in the subsequent steps.

2. Define the implementation of the OCL Standard Library. Map the OCL basic types to basic types in the target language. Map the OCL collection types to collection types in the target language. When needed, define a separate class with (static) collection operations that cannot be mapped to the collection types in the target language. Map each use of an OCL collection iterator to a specially designed code fragment.
3. Define the implementation of the OCL expressions. Take care of evaluation order and possible side effects.
4. Place the code fragments implementing the OCL expressions correctly in the code for the model elements. Define separate operations for each invariant, to be called whenever the invariant needs to be checked.
5. For invariants, and pre- and postconditions, decide when to check them, and what to do when the check fails. Decide whether the constraints need to be checked during runtime.

OCL is a language that can be used to develop platform-independent models; therefore, many design issues need to be addressed during the translation of OCL to code. Once these decisions are made, the translation process is mostly straight-forward. As shown in many of the examples, the OCL code is of a significantly higher level than much of the Java code, making it easier to read and write. This is exactly what is needed when you want to apply MDA techniques to your model.

Chapter 5

Using OCL for MDA

OCL is a small, yet extremely key ingredient for MDA. Without a precise modeling language like OCL, consistent and coherent platform-independent models cannot be made. This chapter describes two other important ways in which OCL fits in with MDA.

5.1 RELATION OF OCL TO MDA

In Section 1.2.3, you learned the building blocks of the MDA framework: models, languages, transformation definitions, and transformation tools. As shown in Figure 5-1, OCL is very helpful in creating at least three of the building blocks:

- Models, because only with a precise specification language can models be built on maturity level 4
- Transformation definitions, because a formal and precise language is needed to write transformation definitions that can be used by automated tools
- Languages, because languages need to be understood within the MDA framework. This is only possible if the language definition is formal and precise.

How to build better models using OCL has been the subject of this book so far. In this chapter, we focus on the second and third aspect of these building blocks: the definition of transformations and modeling languages. For this, we must get to know the metalevel of modeling. This chapter introduces metamodels and metamodeling; explains the UML and OCL metamodels; shows how OCL has helped in the development of these metamodels; and provides an example of a transformation definition written in OCL.

5.2 METAMODELS

The *metamodel* of a language, also known as the *abstract syntax*, is a description of all the concepts that can be used in that language. For instance, the concept

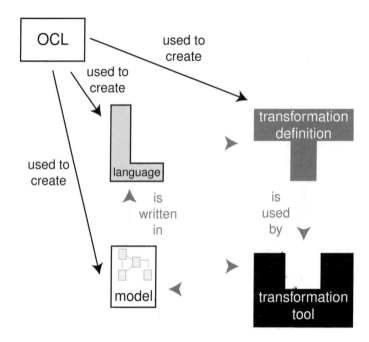

Figure 5-1 *Use of OCL in the MDA framework*

attribute is part of the UML language; the concepts *constructor, method*, and *field* are part of the Java language; and the concepts *table, column*, and *foreign key* are part of the SQL language. These concepts are sometimes called *metaclasses* or *metatypes*. The set of all metaclasses of a language and the relationships between them constitute the metamodel of that language.

Every element of an ordinary model is an instance of a concept in the modeling language used; in other words, every model element is an instance of a metaclass. For instance, in a UML model, a class called *Car* is an instance of the metaclass *Class* from the UML metamodel. An attribute of class *Car*, called *isValuable* of type *Boolean*, is an instance of the metaclass *Attribute* from the UML metamodel. In the model, there is a relation between *Car* and *isValuable*. In the metamodel, this is reflected by the relationship between the metaclass *Class* and the metaclass *Attribute*. Actually, all modelers are familiar with this instance-of relationship: an object named *The Object Constraint Language* is an instance of the class called *Book*. In a metamodel, this relationship is brought one level higher: the class called *Book* is an instance of the metaclass called *Class*. Figure 5-2 shows both instance-of relationships.

As a class defines its objects, a metaclass defines its instances: the model elements. The metaclass *Attribute* from the UML metamodel specifies that an

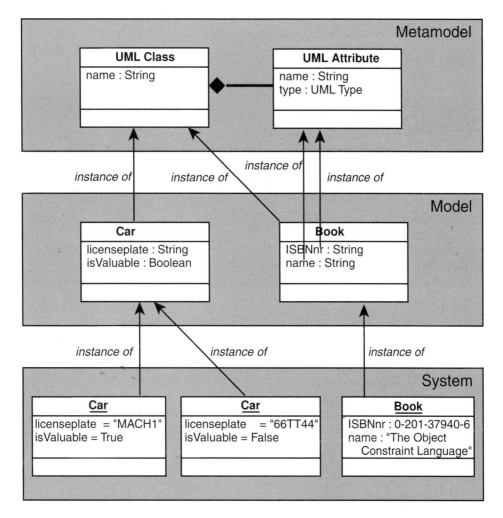

Figure 5-2 *Relation between system, model, and metamodel*

attribute should have a name and a type, e.g., *Boolean*. The metaclass *Class* specifies that each class should have a name, and that it could have attributes, operations, and so on. Each of these related elements must itself be defined within the metamodel; that is, the metaclasses *Attribute* and *Operation* should exist.

A modeler can use in his or her model only elements that are defined by the metamodel of the language the modeler uses. In UML, you can use classes, attributes, associations, states, actions, and so on, because the metamodel of UML contains elements that define what these items are. If the metaclass *Interface* were

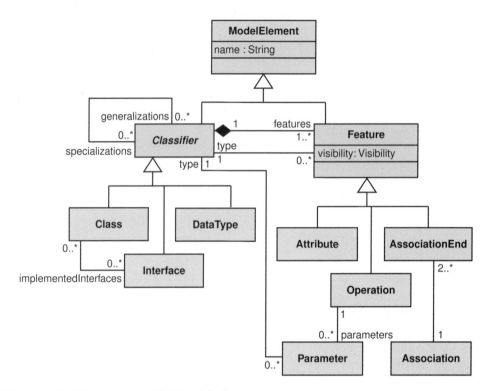

Figure 5-3 *UML metamodel (simplified)*

not included in the UML metamodel, a modeler could not define an interface in a UML model.

5.3 THE OCL AND UML METAMODELS

The OCL and UML metamodels are defined in the OMG standards, and are complete books on their own. The following sections describe only a simplified version of both. They also explain the relationship between them, which will clarify the context of an OCL expression in terms of metaclasses.

5.3.1 The UML Metamodel

A simplified version of part of the UML metamodel is shown in Figure 5-3. It contains the concepts that can be used in a class diagram. Everything in a model is a *ModelElement*, so this is the superclass of all other metaclasses. Also included are types, which in the UML metamodel are called *Classifiers*. *Classifier* is an abstract superclass of the types one may encounter in a model: *Class*, *DataType*, and *Interface* (actually, *Component* should be in this list too). Every classifier has *Features*, either *Attributes*, *Operations*, or *AssociationEnds*. Every feature has a type. For attributes, this is simply the type of the attribute. For operations, this represents the return type. For association ends, the type refers to the class with which the holder of the association end is associated. To define associations, two or more *AssociationEnds* are coupled into one *Association*.

For instance, in the R&L model, the class *LoyaltyProgram* has an association with the class *ProgramPartner*. Both ends of the association have multiplicity 1..*. The end at *LoyaltyProgram* is called *programs*, and the end at *ProgramPartner* is called *partners*. In terms of the metamodel, this means that there are two instances of the metaclass *Class*, called *LoyaltyProgram* and *ProgramPartner*. The *LoyaltyProgram* instance holds an *AssociationEnd* instance called *partners*. The type of this *AssociationEnd* is the instance of metaclass *Class* called *ProgramPartner*.

5.3.2 The OCL Metamodel

A simplified version of part of the OCL metamodel is shown in Figure 5-4. It defines the various types of expressions that can be used. Superclass to all expressions is the metaclass *OclExpression*. The subclass *ModelPropertyCallExp* represents an expression that references a value within the model, an attribute, an operation, or an association end. The metaclass *ModelPropertyCallExp* has three subtypes to indicate the kind of feature of the source that has been called: *AttributeCallExp*, *OperationCallExp*, and *AssociationEndCallExp*. Because properties are always called from some object, a *ModelPropertyCallExp* has a source, which is another *OclExpression*.

For instance, in the following expression, *monkey* is the *OclExpression*, which is the source of the *pealsBanana()* part. The *pealsBanana()* part is an instance of *ModelPropertyCallExp*. In fact, it is an instance of its subclass, *OperationCallExp*:

```
monkey.pealsBanana()
```

Expressions that loop over collections are instances of the metaclass *LoopExpression*. Each loop expression has a source that is a collection or an instance treated as a collection. This source can be written as an OCL expression. The body of a loop expression is the part that indicates which elements of the collection should be considered. For instance, in the following expression, *monkey.siblings* is an OCL expression that represents the source of the *select* loop expression. The part between brackets, *eyes.colour = Colour::blue*, is the body of the loop expression:

```
monkey.siblings->select( eyes.colour = Colour::blue )
```

Although not shown in Figure 5-4, the OCL metamodel adds a number of datatypes to the UML metamodel, such as the *Set*, *OrderedSet*, *Bag*, and *Sequence*

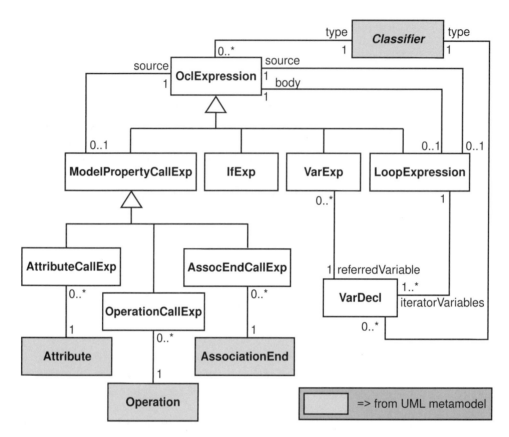

Figure 5-4 *OCL metamodel (simplified) in relation to UML metamodel*

types. Each is a subclass of *Classifier*; in fact they are subclasses of the metaclass *DataType*.

5.3.3 The Relationship Between the UML and OCL Metamodels

The relationship between the UML and OCL metamodels is twofold. First, an OCL expression may reference an element from the model. This element is an instance of a UML metaclass. This relation is shown in Figure 5-4. The metaclasses from the UML metamodel are shown in gray. The associations between the OCL metaclasses and the UML metaclasses define the relationship between the UML and OCL metamodel.

For instance, every OCL expression results in a value. The type of this value is an instance of the UML metaclass *Classifier*. This relationship is represented in the metamodels by the association between the metaclasses *OclExpression* and *Classifier*. Another example is an OCL expression that references an attribute. The

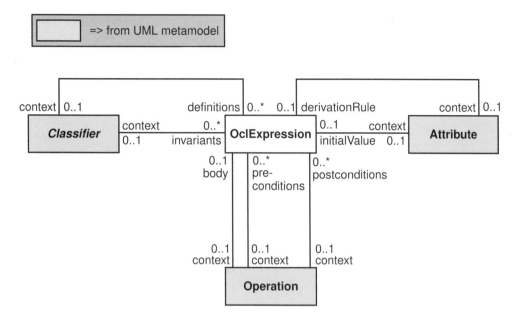

Figure 5-5 *OCL context in terms of the metamodels*

expression is an instance of *AttributeCallExp,* and the attribute is an instance of *Attribute.* Their relationship is represented by the association between both metaclasses.

The second relationship between the UML and OCL metamodels is shown in Figure 5-5. Various elements from the UML metamodel may be adorned with information in the form of an OCL expression. For instance, invariants are *OclExpression* instances that are linked to a *Classifier* instance. This relationship represents the relation between an OCL expression and its context.

For instance, an attribute *A* may have a derivation rule. In terms of the metamodels, the attribute is an instance of the metaclass *Attribute,* and the derivation rule is an instance of the metaclass *OclExpression.* The fact that the rule describes the derivation for attribute *A* is represented in the metamodel by the association with rolename *derivationRule* between the metaclasses *Attribute* and *OclExpression.*

5.4 USING OCL TO DEFINE LANGUAGES

One of the conclusions that may be drawn from the previous sections is that metamodels are simply models. Their only difference is that they reside on another level of abstraction. As OCL is useful in building good models, it is therefore also useful in building good metamodels. When you build a metamodel, you are actually defining a language. Thus, OCL is helpful in defining languages.

In fact, the UML standard was defined using OCL. Approximately two hundred invariants and one hundred operation definitions were written in addition to the diagrams to define the metamodel of UML. In the UML standard, they are called *well-formedness rules*. The following expression, which refers to Figure 5-3, states that an interface may not have any attributes:

```
context Interface
inv: features->select(f |f.oclIsKindOf( Attribute ) )->isEmpty()
```

Even OCL itself was defined using OCL expressions. In the OCL metamodel from Figure 5-4 you can find another example. This one indicates that the source of a loop expression must be a collection, and that the type of the iterator variable must be equal to the type of the elements of the source collection:

```
context LoopExpression
inv: source.oclIsKindOf( Collection )
inv: iteratorVariable.type
              = source.oclAsType(Collection).elementType
```

Within the MDA framework, new languages will need to be defined, but there is also a need for thorough specifications of existing languages. Most programming languages, for instance, are not formally defined. Usually, the only formal part in their specification is the grammar written in a BNF format. For the rest, its users rely on the compilers and the textbooks. In order to use a programming language as PSM language in the MDA, it needs to be defined with at least the same level of formality as UML. This means that for each PSM language, a definition needs to be built in the form of a UML/OCL metamodel.

New languages can also be defined as so-called *profiles* to UML. This means that a completely new metamodel for the language is not needed. Instead, the metamodel of UML is used. Extra rules and a mapping of the language concepts to the syntax used are given. The extra rules, of course, should be stated in OCL.

Existing languages can also be fit within the MDA framework using UML profiles. For instance, there is a Java profile [EJB01]. When you use this profile and draw a diagram that looks like a UML class diagram, you have actually created a number of Java classes.

5.5 USING OCL TO DEFINE TRANSFORMATIONS

A transformation definition describes how a model written in one language can be transformed into a model written in another language. Such a description is generic when it is independent of the actual models. It must make use of the concepts defined in both languages; in other words, it is built using the metaclasses in the metamodels of both languages. A transformation definition relates meta-classes in the source language to metaclasses in the target language.

OCL is useful for defining transformations. An OCL expression is a representation of an element in the model; in this case, in the metamodel. An OCL expression can therefore precisely indicate which element or elements in the source metamodel are used in a certain transformation. The same holds for the elements in the target metamodel. For instance, when a UML class is being transformed into a Java class, not all attributes in the model need to be transformed into class members, only the ones that are owned by the UML class that is being transformed. In OCL, this can be expressed precisely. From the context of the UML class, the attributes to be transformed are exactly identified by the following expression:

```
self.features->select( f | f.isOclType( Attribute ) )
```

Because transformations are to be executed by automated tools, transformation definitions need to be written in a precise and unambiguous manner. Currently, no standard language for writing transformation definitions exists. In our opinion, such a language should be built on the assets of OCL. The next section uses a language that is an extension of OCL to write an example transformation definition.

5.5.1 Example Transformation Definition

This section describes the definition of the transformation of a public attribute to a private attribute and a *get* and *set* operation. Of course, this is only a very simple example, yet it shows how transformations can be defined using OCL expressions. The source and target languages are both UML. The transformation will be executed according to the following rules:

- For each class named *className* in the PIM, there is a class named *className* in the PSM.
- For each public attribute named *attributeName : Type* of class *className* in the PIM the following attributes and operations are part of the class *className* in the target model.

  - A private attribute with the same name: *attributeName : Type*
  - A public operation named with the attribute name, preceded with *'get'* and the attribute type as return type: *getAttributeName() : Type*
  - A public operation named with the attribute name, preceded with *'set'* and with the attribute as parameter and no return value: *setAttributeName(att : Type)*

The preceding rules must be written in a manner that can be understood by an automated tool; therefore, we need to formalize them. To do so, we use a language that is an extension of OCL. In it, each transformation rule is named, and its source and target language are specified. In a rule, a condition may be specified under which the elements of the source language metamodel can or cannot be transformed. Likewise, a condition may be specified that must hold for the generated elements. Finally, the actual transformation is defined by stating the rule to be used to transform a metamodel element of the source language into a metamodel element of the target language. Because there may be conditions in the applied rule, we use the keyword **try** to indicate that the rule will be applied only when the source and target conditions hold. The **<~>** symbol represents the transformation relation:

```
Transformation ClassToClass (UML, UML) {
   source c1: UML::Class;
   target c2: UML::Class;
   source condition -- none
   target condition -- none
   mapping
           try PublicToPrivateAttribute on
                         c1.features <~> c2.features;
           -- everything else remains the same
}
Transformation PublicToPrivateAttribute (UML, UML) {
   source sourceAttribute : UML::Attribute;
   target targetAttribute : UML::Attribute;
           getter           : UML::Operation;
           setter           : UML::Operation;
   source condition
           sourceAttribute.visibility = VisibilityKind::public;
   target condition
         targetAttribute.visibility = VisibilityKind::private
         and -- define the set operation
         setter.name = 'set'.concat(targetAttribute.name)
         and
         setter.parameters->exists( p |
                     p.name = 'new'.concat(targetAttribute.name)
                       and
                     p.type = targetAttribute.type )
         and
         setter.type = OclVoid
         and -- define the get operation
         getter.name = 'get'.concat(targetAttribute.name)
         and
       getter.parameters->isEmpty()
         and
```

```
            getter.returntype = targetAttribute.type;
    mapping
            try StringToString on
                    sourceAttribute.name <~> targetAttribute.name;
            try ClassifierToClassifier on
                    sourceAttribute.type <~> targetAttribute.type;
    }
    -- somewhere the rules StringToString and ClassifierToClassifier
    -- need to be defined
```

Naturally, all details of transformations, and transformation definitions cannot be explained in such a small section. The complete language used to define transformations, an example transformation of a platform-independent model (PIM) to an EJB platform-specific model (PSM), a database PSM, a JSP PSM simultaneously, and much more information on MDA can be found in *MDA Explained, The Model Driven Architecture: Practice and Promise* [Kleppe03].

5.6 SUMMARY

OCL is essential to the application of MDA because it supports the creation of at least three of the MDA building blocks: models, transformation definitions, and languages. Languages are defined by metamodels. The *metamodel* of a language, also known as the *abstract syntax*, is a description of all the concepts that can be used in that language.

You examined simplified versions of the metamodels of both UML and OCL, as well as the relationships between them.

OCL is a very good means to build metamodels—in other words, to define languages, either existing languages that need to be more formally defined, or newly defined languages specified by a UML/OCL metamodel or profile.

OCL is also an excellent tool to define the transformations between PIMs and PSMs, although some extra functionality is necessary. An example of a very simple transformation definition is given. More extensive information on this use of OCL can be found in [Kleppe03].

Part 2

Reference Manual

Chapter 6

The Context of OCL Expressions

This chapter describes the relationship between the UML and OCL parts in a combined model. Much of the information presented here is also described in Chapter 3: Building Models with OCL. Because the current chapter is part of the reference manual we think the descriptions of the constructs in this chapter should be complete, even when this results in some overlap with material in the user manual part of this book.

As in the user manual, all examples in this reference manual refer to the R&L system as depicted in Figure 2-1, unless stated otherwise.

6.1 A COMBINED MODEL

OCL relies on the types (classes, datatypes, and so on) defined in a UML model; thus, using OCL includes the use of (at least some aspects of) UML. Any model in which OCL plays a part consists of some UML diagrams and a series of OCL expressions. Often, only the class diagram is used, but other diagrams may be included in the specification.

A model must be an integrated, consistent entity. In a model, it must be crystal-clear how entities used in one diagram relate to entities in other diagrams. The same holds for the relationship between expressions that are not linked to diagrams, as OCL expressions often are, and entities in the diagrams. You can view this relationship in two ways. First, expressions linked to specific entities may have only specific functions. For instance, an expression defining a new attribute may only be attached to a class, interface, or datatype. Second, the UML model entity to which an expression is linked defines which other model entities are visible and can be referenced. For instance, in an expression attached to a class, all attributes, associations, and query operations of that class may be used.

The link between an entity in a UML diagram and an OCL expression is called the *context definition* of that OCL expression.

6.1.1 The Context of an OCL Expression

The context definition specifies the model entity for which the OCL expression is defined. Usually, this is a class, interface, datatype, or component. Sometimes it is an operation, and only rarely it is an instance. It is always a specific element defined in a UML diagram. This element is called the *context* of the expression.

OCL expressions can be incorporated in the model directly in the diagrams, but they may also be provided in a separate text file. Both cases include a context definition. In the diagram, the context definition is shown by a dotted line that links the model element and the OCL expression. In Figure 6-1, five expressions and their contexts are shown.

When the OCL expression is given in a separate text file, the context definition is given in a textual format. It is denoted by the keyword *context* followed by the name of the type, as shown in the following example invariant:

```
context Customer
inv: name = 'Edward'
```

In addition to the context, it is important to know the contextual type of an expression. The *contextual type* is the type of the object for which the expression will be evaluated. With type, we mean either a class, an interface, a datatype, or a

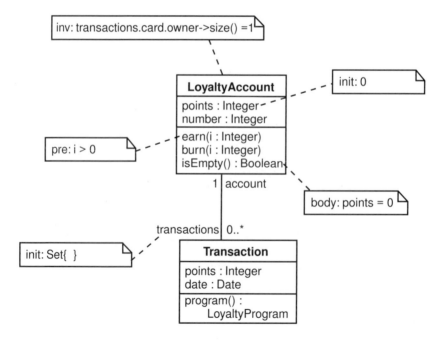

Figure 6-1 *OCL expressions and their context*

component (in terms of the UML standard, a *Classifier*). Note that a package is not instantiable; therefore, it is not a type. When the context itself is a type, the context is equal to the contextual type. When the context is an operation, attribute, or association end, the contextual type is the type for which that feature has been defined. When the OCL expression is connected to an instance in a diagram, the contextual type is the type of that instance.

OCL expressions are evaluated for a single object. This is always an instance of the contextual type. To distinguish between the context and the instance for which the expression is evaluated, the latter is called the *contextual instance*.

OCL expressions can have many different functions, depending on the context of the expression. For instance, when the context is an attribute, the expression may represent an initial value or a derivation rule, but when the context is a class, the expression will never represent an initial value (an initial instance). The remaining sections in this chapter describe the ways in which an OCL expression may be used when connected to various contexts.

6.1.2 The *self* Keyword

Sometimes it is necessary to refer explicitly to the contextual instance. The keyword *self* is used for this purpose. Whenever the reference to the contextual instance is obvious, the use of the keyword *self* is optional. Thus, the previous invariant can be written as follows:

```
context Customer
inv: self.name = 'Edward'
```

The R&L model from Chapter 2 includes an invariant in which the reference to *self* is not optional:

```
context Membership
inv: participants.cards.Membership.includes( self )
```

6.1.3 More Than One Expression to a Context

Often, more than one invariant, or pre- or postcondition, or other type of expression applies to the same context. These can be combined to follow one context definition statement. Because all invariants need to be true for an instance of the class, the invariants are conceptually connected by the *Boolean and* operation. The same holds for sets of pre- and postconditions. Therefore, the following two examples have exactly the same meaning:

```
context Customer
inv: self.name = 'Edward'
inv: self.title = 'Mr.'
```

```
context Customer
inv: self.name = 'Edward' and self.title = 'Mr.'
```

The following two sets of pre- and postconditions have the same meaning as well:

```
context LoyaltyProgram::addService(p: ProgramPartner,
                                   l: ServiceLevel,
                                   s: Service)
pre: partners->includes( p )
pre: levels->includes( l )
post: partners.deliveredServices->includes( s )
post: levels.availableServices->includes( s )

context LoyaltyProgram::addService(p: ProgramPartner,
                                   l: ServiceLevel,
                                   s: Service)
pre: partners->includes( p ) and levels->includes( l )
post: partners.deliveredServices->includes( s ) and
               levels.availableServices->includes( s )
```

6.2 CLASSES AND OTHER TYPES

This section explains which function expressions may have when the context is a type, i.e., a class, interface, datatype, or component. The model elements that may be used in this case are all attributes, query operations, states, and associations of the type.

6.2.1 Invariants

The first way in which an expression with a type as context can be used is as an invariant. An invariant is described using a boolean expression that evaluates to true if the invariant is met. The invariant must be true upon completion of the constructor and completion of every public operation, but not necessarily during the execution of operations. Incorporating an invariant in a model means that any system made according to the model is faulty when the invariant is broken. How to react when an invariant is broken is explained in Section 4.6.2.

To indicate that the expression is intended to be an invariant, the context declaration is followed by the keyword *inv*, an optional name, and a colon, as shown in the following example:

```
context Customer
inv myInvariant23: self.name = 'Edward'
```

Using an OCL expression as invariant means that for all instances of the contextual type, the expression must evaluate to true. Thus, in our (contrived) example, all instances of class *Customer* would have to be named Edward.

An invariant may be named, which can be useful for reference in an accompanying text. The preceding invariant is named *myInvariant23*.

6.2.2 Definitions of Attributes or Operations

Attributes or operations may be defined by an OCL expression. Defining an attribute or operation this way means that every instance of the contextual type holds an attribute or operation that conforms to the given definition.

The context of an attribute or operation definition is always the type that must hold the new element. To indicate that the expression is intended to be a definition, the context declaration is followed by the keyword *def* and a colon, as shown in the following examples. The second example, by the way, is a specification of the operation used in the use case example described in Section 3.8.1:

```
context Customer
def: initial : String = name.substring(1,1)

context CustomerCard
def: getTotalPoints( d: Date ) : Integer =
        transactions->select( date.isAfter(d) ).points->sum()
```

In the case of an attribute definition, the name and type of the attribute must be given. The expression following the equal sign is also mandatory. This expression indicates how the value of the attribute must be calculated. It is a derivation rule (see Section 6.3.1).

All operations defined by an OCL expression are considered to be query operations. The name, parameters (including their types), and the return type (if any) of the operation must be given. The expression following the equal sign is also mandatory, and states the result of the operation (see Section 6.4.2).

6.3 ATTRIBUTES AND ASSOCIATION ENDS

This section explains which functions expressions may have when the context is an attribute or the role of one end of an association. The model elements that may be used in this case are all attributes, query operations, states, and associations of the contextual type.

6.3.1 Derivation Rules

An expression whose context is an attribute or association role may be used as a *derivation rule*. A derivation rule specifies that the value of the context element should always be equal to the value given by the evaluation of the derivation rule. If the context is an attribute, the contextual type is the type that holds the attribute. If the context is an association end, the contextual type is the type at the opposite end of the association. For example, in the R&L model, the context of the association end named *participants* is the class *LoyaltyProgram*.

To indicate that the expression is intended to be a derivation rule, the context declaration includes the name of the attribute or the association end, and is followed by the keyword *derive* and a colon, as shown in the following examples:

```
context LoyaltyAccount::totalPointsEarned : Integer
derive: transactions->select( oclIsTypeOf( Earning ) )
            .points->sum()

context CustomerCard::myLevel : ServiceLevel
derive: Membership.currentLevel
```

6.3.2 Initial Values

The initial value of an attribute or association role can also be given by an OCL expression. An initial value is the value that the attribute or association end will have at the moment that the contextual instance is created. The context declaration is followed by the keyword *init*, the name of the attribute, and the expression that gives the initial value, as shown in the following two examples:

```
context CustomerCard::transactions : Set( Transaction )
init: Set{}

context CustomerCard::valid : Boolean
init: true
```

Note the difference between an initial value and a derivation rule. A derivation rule states an invariant: The derived element should always have the same value that the rule expresses. An initial value must hold only at the moment when the contextual instance is created. After that moment, the attribute may have a different value at any point in time.

6.4 OPERATIONS

This section explains the different functions which expressions may have for operations in the model. The model elements that may be used in an expression whose context is an operation are all attributes, query operations, states, and associations of the contextual type, plus the parameters of the operation.

6.4.1 Preconditions and Postconditions

The first two ways in which expressions may be used for operations are pre- and postconditions: two forms of constraints. A precondition is a boolean expression that must be true at the moment when the operation starts its execution. A postcondition is a boolean expression that must be true at the moment when the operation ends its execution. A precondition specifies that the expression must evaluate to true; otherwise, the operation will not be executed. The meaning of a postcondition specifies that the expression must evaluate to true; otherwise, the operation has not executed correctly.

The context is denoted by the keyword *context* followed by the name of the type to which the operation belongs; a double colon; the complete operation signature—that is, the name of the operation; all parameters and their types; and the return type of the operation. Usually, the complete operation signature is defined in the UML class diagram.

Following this context definition are lines—labeled with the keywords *pre*: and *post*:—that contain the actual pre- and postconditions, respectively. The general syntax looks like the following:

```
context Type1::operation(arg : Type2) : ReturnType
pre  : -- some expression using the param arg and features of the
         -- contextual type
post: -- some expression using the param arg, features of the
         -- contextual type, the @pre keyword, and messaging
         -- expressions
```

The contextual instance is always an instance of the type for which the operation has been defined.

Note that in contrast to invariants, which must always be true, pre- and postconditions need be true only at a certain point in time: before and after execution of an operation, respectively.

6.4.2 Body of Query Operations

Query operations can be fully defined by specifying the result of the operation in a single expression. By definition, query operations have no side effects. Execution of a query operation results in a value or set of values, nothing more. The context is indicated in the same manner as for pre- and postconditions. Instead of the keywords *pre* or *post*, the keyword *body* is used, followed by the body expression:

```
context CustomerCard::getTransactions(from : Date, until: Date )
                          : Set(Transaction)
body: transactions->select( date.isAfter( from ) and
                            date.isBefore( until ) )
```

6.5 EXPRESSIONS IN BEHAVIOR DIAGRAMS

This section explains the way in which expressions may be used in UML behavior diagrams. The model elements that may be used in an expression in a behavior diagram are all attributes, query operations, states, and associations of the contextual type. What the contextual type is depends on the position of the expression in the diagram, as explained in the following sections.

6.5.1 Instances

An interaction diagram shows the lifelines of instances. In an activity diagram, a number of activities may be executed by a specific instance. To indicate which instances are depicted and their mutual relationships, OCL expressions can be used. The context of these expressions is the diagram in which they occur. The contextual instance can be any instance in the system. Note that it is good practice to state the contextual instance explicitly. The contextual type is the type of the contextual instance.

6.5.2 Conditions

A message in a sequence or collaboration diagram can have an attached condition that specifies in what circumstances the message is sent. This condition can be written as an OCL expression. In this case, the OCL expression is linked to an instance, not to a type. The contextual instance is the instance that sends the message, the source. The context is the message. The contextual type is the type of the contextual instance.

Conditions may also be part of activity diagrams. In this case, the contextual instance is the instance that executes the overall activity, as specified by the complete diagram. The context is the decision node. The contextual type is the type of the contextual instance.

6.5.3 Guards

OCL expressions can be used to express guards in statecharts. The context is the transition for which the guard is defined. A guard is included in the statechart diagram itself. It is written between square brackets ([and]) before the event coupled to a transition. The contextual type for a guard is the type to which the statechart belongs. The contextual instance is the instance of the contextual type for which a transition fires.

6.5.4 Actual Parameter Values

Messages in collaboration and sequence diagrams can take parameters. Because a message represents an operation call these parameters are actual values. You can specify the actual value of such a parameter using an OCL expression. The context of the expression is the message. The contextual instance is the instance that sends the message. The contextual type is the type of the contextual instance.

Note that a message to an object in an interaction diagram must conform to an operation in the type of the target object, or to a signal that has been elsewhere defined. Likewise, the result message in an interaction diagram must conform to the type indicated as the result type of the called operation.

Actions in statechart or activity diagrams can take parameters too. Like the parameters to messages in an interaction diagram, these are actual values that can be specified using an OCL expression. The context of the expression is the action. Note that the parameter values must conform to the operation called, or the signal sent. As with guards, the contextual type is the type to which the statechart belongs, and the contextual instance is the instance of the contextual type that executes the action.

6.5.5 Target to Actions or Activities

An action in a statechart represents either an operation call or the sending of an event. An action is targeted at a specific object or set of objects. An OCL expression can be used to identify the target of an action. Actions may be linked to either transitions or states in a statechart. The context of the expression is the transition or state to which the action is linked. The contextual instance is the instance that executes the transition.

An activity in an activity diagram may also represent an operation call. The target of this call can be specified by an OCL expression, in a similar fashion to the targets in a statechart. The context in this case is the activity. The contextual instance is the instance that executes the overall activity, as specified by the complete diagram. In both diagrams, the contextual type is the type of the contextual instance.

6.5.6 Change Events

A *change event* is generated when one or more attributes or associations change value according to an expression. The event occurs whenever the value of the expression changes from false to true. A change event is denoted in the statechart by the keyword *when*, followed by the expression.

The condition of the change event can be written in OCL. The context of the expression is the transition. As with guards, the contextual type is the type to which the statechart belongs.

6.6 USE CASES

In UML use cases, pre- and postconditions may be used. These may also be written using OCL. Because use cases are an informal way of stating requirements, and OCL is a formal language, some adjustments need to be made when the pre- and postconditions of use cases are defined using OCL expressions.

6.6.1 Preconditions and Postconditions

Although use cases can be considered to be operations defined on the complete system, you cannot identify the complete system as a type, because it is neither a class, an interface, a datatype, or a component. Therefore, the pre- and postconditions of a use case have no contextual type or contextual instance. As a consequence, the keyword *self* cannot be used.

Another consequence is that it is not clear which model elements may be referenced in the expression. Normally, all elements held by the contextual type may be used. Here, there is no contextual type. The model elements that may be used must be explicitly stated. This can be done by formalizing the types mentioned in the use case, e.g., *Customer* and *Order*, in an accompanying class diagram, and adding to the use case template a section called *concerns* with a list of variable declarations, e.g., *newCustomer : Customer, newOrder : Order*.

Yet another consequence is that you cannot write a context definition, as there is no contextual type to be referenced. The OCL expressions may be included in the use case at the position indicated by the use case template.

6.7 CONSTRAINTS AND INHERITANCE

No explicit rules in the UML standard explain whether an expression on a superclass is inherited by its subclasses. To use expressions in a meaningful way in a situation where inheritance plays a role, you need to give them proper semantics. The most widely accepted semantics of inheritance is to ensure that any instance of a subclass must behave the same as any instance of its superclass—as far as anyone or any program using the superclass can tell. This principle, called Liskov's Substitution Principle [Liskov94], is defined as follows:

> *Wherever an instance of a class is expected, one can always substitute an instance of any of its subclasses.*

OCL expressions adhere to this principle. This section describes the consequences thereof for invariants, preconditions, and postconditions.

6.7.1 Consequences for Invariants

The invariants put on the superclass must always apply to the subclass too; otherwise, the substitution principle cannot be safely applied. The subclass may strengthen the invariant, because then the superclass invariant will still hold. The general rule for invariants is as follows:

> *An invariant for a superclass is inherited by its subclasses. A subclass may strengthen the invariant but cannot weaken it.*

In the model shown in Figure 6-2, we can define for the superclass *Stove* an invariant that specifies that its temperature must not be hotter than 200 degrees Celsius:

```
context Stove
inv: temperature <= 200
```

It would be dangerous if a subclass *ElectricStove* could exceed that maximum. For example, suppose that *ElectricStove* could have a temperature no hotter than 300 degrees Celsius:

```
context ElectricStove
inv: temperature <= 300
```

ElectricStove cannot be used safely in some places where *Stove* can be used. If you have a location that is fire-safe up to 250 degrees Celsius, you know you can safely put a *Stove* there. If you place a *Stove* at this location and the *Stove* happens to be an *ElectricStove*, the place may be set on fire—definitely not a good idea.

Under some circumstances, Liskov's Substitution Principle looks too restrictive. Subclasses may change superclass operations and add their own attributes and operations. In some cases, the superclass invariants should be changed to correspond with these alterations. Whether or not an invariant on a superclass needs

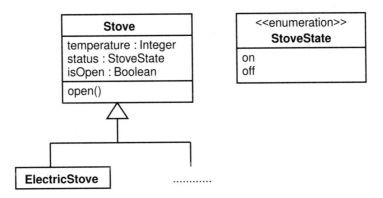

Figure 6-2 *Inheritance of invariants*

to be changed when a new subclass is added depends on the reason for and contents of the invariant.

Consider again the *Stove* example. If the invariant on the temperature is put on the *Stove* because its surroundings would catch fire if the temperature were too high, then a new subclass cannot weaken the invariant. Conversely, if the invariant is put on the *Stove* because of the materials used in the construction, then the invariant might be changed when a new subclass uses more fireproof materials. Thus, using the subclass would be safer, even when the invariant on the temperature is weakened. In this case, we recommend rewriting the temperature invariant so that it includes information about the materials used to construct the stove. This approach states the intention of the invariant more cleanly and removes the need to redefine it for each subclass.

6.7.2 Consequences for Preconditions and Postconditions

When an operation is redefined in a subclass, do the pre- and postconditions of the original operation in the superclass still apply? To find the answer, view the pre- and postconditions as the contract for the operation (see Section 3.3.5). The design by contract principle follows Liskov's Substitution Principle. The rules for pre- and postconditions are as follows:

> *A precondition may be weakened, not strengthened, in a redefinition of an operation in a subclass.*

> *A postcondition may be strengthened, not weakened, in a redefinition of an operation in a subclass.*

The following example illustrates these rules. We define the operation *open()* for the class *Stove* in Figure 6-2 as follows:

```
context Stove::open()
pre : status = StoveState::off
post: status = StoveState::off and isOpen
```

This means that we expect to be able to open a *Stove* when its status is *off*. After we have opened the *Stove*, we expect its status to be *off*, and *isOpen* to be true. Suppose for the subclass *ElectricStove* we redefine *open()* and give it different pre- and postconditions:

```
context ElectricStove::open()
pre : status = StoveState::off and temperature <= 100
post: isOpen
```

The precondition of the redefined *open()* includes an extra condition *(temperature <= 100)*. The consequence is that *ElectricStove* does not behave like a *Stove* anymore, because it won't be able to open under the conditions in which a *Stove* will open *(status = StoveState::off)*. If we want to make sure that an *ElectricStove* can be substituted for a *Stove*, the precondition for the redefined *open()* cannot be strengthened. We could weaken the precondition, however, because then it will still work as expected for *Stove*.

The postcondition of *open()* in *ElectricStove* is weakened, because the condition *status = StoveState::off* has been removed. The consequence is that the *ElectricStove* won't fulfill the expectations of a *Stove*. After opening, the stove should be in status *off*. We could have strengthened the postcondition, because then the original expectation would still be met.

Chapter 7

Basic OCL Elements

This chapter describes the basic elements with which you can write constraints. These basic elements can be used without any reference to the elements in the UML model.

7.1 EXPRESSIONS, TYPES, AND VALUES

In OCL, each value, whether it is an object, a component instance, or a datavalue, has a certain type, which defines the operations that can be applied to the object. Types in OCL are divided into the following groups:

- Predefined types, as defined in the standard library, including the following:
  - Basic types
  - Collection types
- User-defined types

The predefined basic types are *Integer*, *Real*, *String*, and *Boolean*, which are described in this chapter in some detail. Their definitions are similar to those in many known languages.

The predefined collection types are *Collection*, *Set*, *Bag*, *OrderedSet*, and *Sequence*. They are used to specify the exact results of a navigation through associations in a class diagram. You need to be familiar with these types to write more complex expressions. Collection types, and how to use them, are described in Chapter 9.

User-defined types, such as *Customer* or *LoyaltyProgram*, are defined by the user in the UML diagrams. Every instantiable model element—that is, each class, interface, component, or datatype—in a UML diagram is automatically a type in OCL. Chapter 8 explains how to work with user-defined types in OCL expressions.

Each OCL expression represents a value; therefore, it has a type as well—either a user-defined type or a predefined OCL type. Each OCL expression has a result:

the value that results from evaluating the expression. The type of the result value is equal to the type of the expression.

7.1.1 Value Types and Object Types

OCL distinguishes between value types and object types. Both are types, i.e., both specify instances, but there is one important difference: *value types* define instances that never change. The integer 1, for example, will never change its value and become an integer with a value of 2. *Object types*, or Classifiers, represent types that define instances that can change their value(s). An instance of the class *Person* can change the value of its attribute *name* and still remain the same instance. Other names have been used to indicate the same difference. For instance, Martin Fowler [Fowler97] calls object types *reference objects,* and value types *value objects.*

Another important characteristic of value types involves identity. For value types, the value identifies the instance, hence the name. Two occurrences of a value type that have the same value are by definition one and the same instance. Two occurrences of an object type are the same instance only if they have the same (object) identity. In other words, value types have value-based identity; object types have reference-based identity.

Both the predefined basic types and the predefined collection types of OCL are value types. The user-defined types can be either value types or object types. UML datatypes, including enumeration types, are value types. UML classes, components, and interfaces are object types.

7.2 BASIC TYPES AND OPERATORS

The following sections define the basic predefined types and their operations. Basic types are typically not very interesting to read about, so this section is deliberately kept short. It explains only the more interesting operations of the basic types, those that differ from the ones in most programming languages and therefore offer some surprises.

7.2.1 The *Boolean* Type

A value of *Boolean* type can only be one of two values: *true* or *false*. The operations defined on *Boolean* include all the familiar ones, shown in Table 7-1. A standard operation on the *Boolean* type that is uncommon to most programming languages—but often encountered in a more theoretical environment or in specification languages—is the *implies* operation. This operation states that the result of the total expression is true if it is the case that when the first boolean operand is true, the second *Boolean* operand is also true. If the first boolean operand is false, the whole *implies* expression always evaluates to true.

Table 7-1 *Standard operations for the* Boolean *type*

Operation	Notation	Result Type
or	a or b	Boolean
and	a and b	Boolean
exclusive or	a xor b	Boolean
negation	not a	Boolean
equals	a = b	Boolean
not equals	a <> b	Boolean
implies	a implies b	Boolean

Take as an example the class *Service* from the R&L example. The result of the following sample expression is true if for every service it can be said that when it offers bonus points it never burns bonus points. In other words, a customer cannot earn bonus points, when using a service that is bought with bonus points:

```
context Service
inv: self.pointsEarned > 0 implies not (self.pointsBurned = 0)
```

Another interesting operation on the *Boolean* type is the if-then-else. It is denoted in the following manner:

```
if <boolean OCL expression>
then <OCL expression>
else <OCL expression>
endif
```

The result value of an *if-then-else* operation is the result of either the OCL expression in the *then* clause or the OCL expression in the *else* clause, depending on the result of the boolean expression in the *if* clause. You cannot omit the *else* clause of the expression because an OCL expression must result in a value. Omitting the *else* clause causes the expression to result in an undefined state if the boolean OCL expression in the *if* clause is false. Both OCL expressions within the *else* and the *then* clauses must be of the same type.

Here are some other examples of valid boolean expressions:

```
not true
age() > 21 and age() < 65
age() <= 12 xor cards->size() > 3
```

Table 7-2 *Standard operations for the* Integer *and* Real *types*

Operation	Notation	Result Type
equals	a = b	Boolean
not equals	a <> b	Boolean
less	a < b	Boolean
more	a > b	Boolean
less or equal	a <= b	Boolean
more or equal	a >= b	Boolean
plus	a + b	Integer or Real
minus	a - b	Integer or Real
multiplication	a * b	Integer or Real
division	a / b	Real
modulus	a.mod(b)	Integer
integer division	a.div(b)	Integer
absolute value	a.abs()	Integer or Real
maximum of a and b	a.max(b)	Integer or Real
minimum of a and b	a.min(b)	Integer or Real
round	a.round()	Integer
floor	a.floor()	Integer

```
title = 'Mr.' or title = 'Ms.'
name = 'Foobar'
if standard = 'UML'
    then 'using UML standard'
    else 'watch out: non UML features'
endif
```

7.2.2 The *Integer* and *Real* Types

The *Integer* type in OCL represents the mathematical natural numbers. Because OCL is a modeling language, there are no restrictions on the integer values; in particular, there is no such thing as a maximum integer value. In the same way,

Table 7-3 *Standard operations for the* String *type*

Operation	Expression	Result Type
concatenation	string.concat(string)	String
size	string.size()	Integer
to lower case	string.toLower()	String
to upper case	string.toUpper()	String
substring	string.substring(int,int)	String
equals	string1 = string2	Boolean
not equals	string1 <> string2	Boolean

the *Real* type in OCL represents the mathematical concept of real values. As in mathematics, *Integer* is a subtype of *Real*.

For the *Integer* and *Real* types, the usual operations apply: addition, subtraction, multiplication, and division. For both the *Integer* and the *Real* types, there is an additional operation, *abs,* that provides the absolute value of the given value; for example, *-1.abs()* results in 1, and *(2.4).abs()* results in 2.4. An additional operator on the *Real* type is the *floor* operator, which rounds the real value down to an integer number; for example, *(4.6).floor()* results in an integer instance with the value 4. The *round* operation on a real value results in the closest integer; for example, *(4.6).round()* results in the *Integer* 5. An overview of all operations on integer and real values is provided in Table 7-2.

The following examples illustrate the *Real* and *Integer* types. All these examples are expresssions of the *Boolean* type, which result in true:

```
2654 * 4.3 + 101 = 11513.2
(3.2).floor() / 3 = 1
1.175 * (-8.9).abs() - 10 = 0.4575
12 > 22.7 = false
12.max(33) = 33
33.max(12) = 33
13.mod(2) = 1
13.div(2) = 6
33.7.min(12) = 12.0
-24.abs() = 24
(-2.4).floor() = -3
```

7.2.3 The *String* Type

Strings are sequences of characters. Literal strings are written with enclosing single quotes, such as *'apple'* or *'weird cow'*. The operations available on *Strings* are *toUpper, toLower, size, substring,* and *concat* (see Table 7-3).

The following examples illustrate the *String* type. All these examples are expressions of the *Boolean* type, and result in true:

```
'Anneke'.size() = 6
('Anneke' = 'Jos') = false
'Anneke '.concat('and Jos') = 'Anneke and Jos'
'Anneke'.toUpper() = 'ANNEKE'
'Anneke'.toLower() = 'anneke'
'Anneke and Jos'.substring(12, 14) = 'Jos'
```

7.3 PRECEDENCE RULES

With so many operations available on an instance of a type, rules are needed to determine the precedence of the operations. Table 7-4 shows the OCL operations, starting with the highest precedence. In case of doubt, the use of parentheses () is always allowed to specify the precedence explicitly.

Table 7-4 *Precedence for OCL operations (highest to lowest)*

Name	Syntax
Pathname	::
Time expression	@pre
The dot, arrow, and message operations	., ->, ^, ^^
Unary operations	-, not
Multiplication and division	*, /
Addition and substraction	+, -
Relational operations	<, >, <=, >=, <>, =
Logical operations	and, or, xor
Logical implies	implies

7.4 USE OF INFIX OPERATORS

The use of *infix operators* is allowed in OCL. The operators +, -, *, /, <, >, <>, <=, and >= are used as infix operators. If a user-defined type includes one of those operators with the correct signature, it will also be used as an infix operator. The correct signature includes only one parameter of the same type as the contextual instance. For the infix operators <, >, <=, >=, <>, *and*, *or*, and *xor*, the return type must be *Boolean*. For the infix operators +, -, *, and /, the return type must be equal to the type of the contextual instance.

Conceptually, the following two expressions are completely equal; both invoke the + operation on *a*, with *b* as the parameter to the operation. The second notation is not allowed:

```
a + b
a.+(b)
```

7.5 COMMENTS

OCL expressions can contain *comments*. An OCL line comment begins with two hyphens. All text from the hyphens to the end of the line is considered to be a comment. Comments longer than one line may be enclosed between /* and */. For example, the following lines contain valid OCL expressions:

```
-- the expression 20 * 5 + 4 should be evaluated here

20 * 5 + 4 -- this is a comment

/* this is a very long comment that does not enlighten the reader
one bit about what the expression is really about */
```

The following line is not a valid OCL expression:

```
20 * -- this is a comment 5 + 4
```

Chapter 8

User-defined Types

This chapter describes all the OCL constructs that refer to information in user-defined types.

8.1 FEATURES OF USER-DEFINED TYPES

When a user-defined type is specified in an UML diagram, a number of features of that type are given. The features of a user-defined type include the following:

- Attributes
- Operations
- Class attributes
- Class operations
- Association ends that are derived from associations and aggregations[1]

Each feature can be used in an OCL expression. This section explains how the first four features may be used. Section 8.2 explains how to use the information in an association.

8.1.1 Attributes and Operations

Attributes of user-defined types may be used in expressions by writing a dot followed by the attribute name. As with attributes, the operations of user-defined types can be used in OCL expressions. However, note one fundamental restriction: Because OCL is a side-effect-free language, operations that change the state of any object are not allowed. Only so-called *query operations*, which return a value but don't change anything, can be used. According to the UML specification, each operation has a boolean label called *isQuery*. If this label is true, the operation has no side effects and can be used in OCL expressions.

---

[1] Note that inheritance relationships cannot be navigated, because they don't represent relationships between instances.

The dot notation used to reference attributes is also used to reference operations. The name of the operation, however, is always followed by two parentheses, which enclose the optional arguments of the operation. Even if an operation
has no arguments, the parentheses are mandatory. This is necessary to distinguish
between attributes and operations, because UML allows attributes and operations
to have identical names.

The visibility of attributes and operations is ignoredby default in OCL. Option-
ally OCL can use the rules given in the UML specification. In this case, a private
attribute of an associated object may not be used in an OCL expression, because it
is not visible to the contextual instance.

8.1.2 Class Operations and Attributes

Class operations and class attributes may also be used in OCL expressions. The
syntax for referencing a class attribute or operation is the class name followed by
two colons, followed by the attribute or operation name (and parameters). For
example, in the R&L example shown in Figure 2-1, the attribute *now* of *Date* is a
class attribute. It can be used as shown in the following example:

```
context CustomerCard
inv: goodThru.isAfter( Date::now )
```

8.2 ASSOCIATIONS AND AGGREGATIONS

Another feature of a user-defined type that you can use within OCL is derived
from the associations in the class model. Every association has a number of association ends. Each end has a multiplicity, a type to which it is connected, and an
optional ordering marker; it may also have a name. This name is called a *rolename*.
Conceptually, an association end is or defines a feature of the class connected to
the other end(s) of the association.

Association ends can be used to navigate from one object in the system to
another. Therefore, the conceptual features that they define are sometimes called
navigations. If the name of the association end is missing, the name of the connected type may be used. If using the typename results in an ambiguity, the specification of a rolename is mandatory. The same is true for associations that are
marked to be aggregations. In Figure 8-1, which shows part of the Royal and
Loyal model, *Customer* has two navigations: *programs* and *cards*. Class *Customer-*
Card has one navigation named *owner.* Class *LoyaltyProgram* also has one navigation named *customer.*

Navigations in OCL are treated as attributes. The dot-notation used to reference attributes is also used to reference navigations. In one type, all names,

whether attribute names or navigation names, must be unique. This arrangement prevents ambiguities between attribute and navigation names.

The type of a navigation is either a user-defined type or a collection of user-defined types. If the multiplicity of the association end is at most one, the result type is the user-defined type connected to the association end. If the multiplicity is greater than one, the result is a collection. The elements in the collection must all be of, or conform to, the user-defined type connected to the association end. In our example, the result type of the *owner* navigation from *CustomerCard* is a user-defined type: *Customer.* The result type of both the navigations *programs* and *cards* from *Customer* are collections; in this case, (unordered) *Sets.* If the association end had been marked *{ordered}*, the result type would have been *OrderedSet.* The differences between sets, ordered sets, bags, and sequences are described in Section 9.1.

For the diagram in Figure 8-1, we can define an invariant that uses the *owner* navigation from the context of *CustomerCard.* Because this OCL expression results in a value of type *Customer,* all attributes and operations on *Customer* that are visible to the contextual instance are now available for use in the remainder of the expression, as shown in the following example:

```
context CustomerCard
inv: self.owner.dateOfBirth.isBefore( Date::now )
```

The same holds for navigations defined on the *Customer* type that are visible to the contextual instance; they may be used in the remainder of the expressions as well:

```
context CustomerCard
inv: self.owner.programs->size() > 0
```

The result of navigating more than one association with multiplicity *many* is by definition a value of type *Bag.* If one of the navigations in the series is marked *{ordered}*, the result is a value of type *Sequence.*

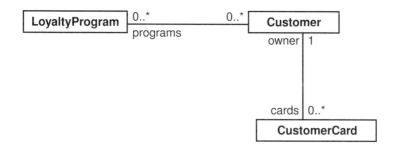

Figure 8-1 *Navigations*

When we combine navigations, we have the means to navigate through the complete class diagram. From the context of one class in the class diagram, we can write constraints on all connected classes. Surely, this is not good practice. The question of when and how to use navigations is addressed in Section 3.10.2.

8.2.1 Association Classes

A UML class diagram enables us to define *association classes*, which are classes attached to an association. From an association class, you can always navigate to the instances of the classes at all ends of the association, using the same rules for naming as for normal navigations, for binary as well as multiple assocations. Note that, because of the nature of an association class, such a navigation always results in one single value and never in a collection of any kind.

The R&L model (see Figure 8-2) has one association class: *Membership*. This class has three navigations: *programs* of type *LoyaltyProgram*, *participants* of type *Customer*, and—because of the extra association—*currentLevel* of type *ServiceLevel*. The following invariant states that the actual service level of a membership must always be a service level of the loyalty program to which the membership belongs:

```
context Membership
inv: programs.levels->includes( currentLevel )
```

It is also possible to navigate in the other direction: from the associated classes to the association class. In the R&L model, we can navigate from *Customer* and *Loyal-*

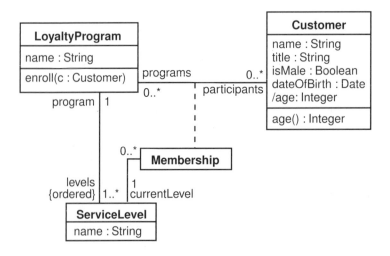

Figure 8-2 *Association class from the UML diagram*

tyProgram to *Membership*. Because an association class cannot have a rolename, the navigation name is the name of the association class. Note that the previous version of OCL required that the class name be written starting with a lowercase letter. In version 2.0, the name used should be identical to the name of the association class.

The multiplicity on the association ends is used to determine the type of the expression. If from a certain context the multiplicity on the opposite end is more than one, then the navigation to the association class will result in a collection of association class instances. If the multiplicity is not greater than one, then the navigation to the association class will result in one association class instance. For example, navigating from *Customer* to *Membership* will result in a value of type *Set(LoyaltyProgram)*.

The following invariant makes a statement similar to the preceding one, but from the context of the *LoyaltyProgram*: the set of service levels must include the set of all actual levels of all memberships. Note that from the context of *LoyaltyProgram*, the expression *Membership.currentLevel* is of type *Bag(ServiceLevel)*; therefore, we use the operation *includesAll* instead of *includes*:

```
context LoyaltyProgram
inv: levels->includesAll( Membership.currentLevel )
```

8.2.2 Qualified Associations

In a UML class diagram, you can use *qualified associations*. Qualified associations can be used in OCL expressions in the same way that normal associations are used. The only difference is that we need a way to indicate the value of the qualifier in the expression. The syntax used for qualified associations is

```
object.navigation[qualifierValue, ...]
```

If there are multiple qualifiers, their values are separated by commas. You can navigate to all associated objects by not specifying a qualifier. This is identical to navigation of normal associations.

Figure 8-3 shows an alternative class diagram for the R&L model. The ordered association from *LoyaltyProgram* to *ServiceLevel* is replaced by an association with the qualifier *levelNumber*. This means that for each combination of a *LoyaltyProgram* and a *levelNumber*, there is zero or one *ServiceLevel*. The *levelNumber* specifies the order of the *ServiceLevels*. To specify that the name of the *ServiceLevel* with *levelNumber* 1 must be *'basic'*, we can write the following invariant:

```
context LoyaltyProgram
inv: self.levels[1].name = 'basic'
```

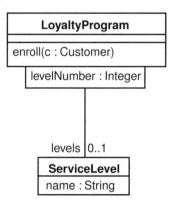

Figure 8-3 *Qualified association in the UML diagram*

If we want to state that there is at least one *ServiceLevel* with the name *'basic'*, disregarding the *levelNumber*, we can state the following invariant:

```
context LoyaltyProgram
inv: self.levels->exists(name = 'basic')
```

The first part, *self.serviceLevel*, is the collection of all *ServiceLevels* associated with the *LoyaltyProgram*. The *exists* operation states that at least one of those service levels must have its *name* attribute equal to *'basic'*.

8.3 ENUMERATION TYPES

An *enumeration type* is a special user-defined type often used as a type for attributes. It is defined within the UML class diagram by using the enumeration stereotype, as shown in Figure 8-4. The values defined in the enumeration can be used as values within an OCL expression. The notation to indicate one of the enumeration values in an OCL expression is the enumeration type name, two colons, followed by the enumeration value identifier. Note that the previous version of OCL used a different notation.

In Figure 8-4, the *Customer* class is shown again. Now we have changed the attribute *isMale* to an attribute *gender*. The following invariant states that male *Customers* must be approached using the title *'Mr.'*.

```
context Customer
inv: gender = Gender::male implies title = 'Mr.'
```

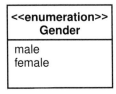

Figure 8-4 Customer *class with enumeration*

The only operators available on enumeration values are the equality and inequality operators. They are denoted by = and <>, respectively.

Chapter 9

Collection Types

This chapter describes the collection types that are part of the OCL standard library, and the way they can be used in expressions.

9.1 THE COLLECTION TYPES

In object-oriented systems, the manipulation of collections (of objects) is very common. Because one-to-one associations are rare, most associations define a relationship between one object and a collection of other objects. To enable you to manipulate these collections, OCL predefines a number of types for dealing with collections, sets, and so on.

Within OCL, there are five collection types. Four of them—the *Set*, *OrderedSet*, *Bag*, and *Sequence* types—are concrete types and can be used in expressions. The fifth, the *Collection* type, is the abstract supertype of the other four and is used to define the operations common to all collection types. In this book, we refer to *Set*, *OrderedSet*, *Bag*, and *Sequence* as the collection types.

The four concrete collection types are defined as follows:

- A *Set* is a collection that contains instances of a valid OCL type. A set does not contain duplicate elements; any instance can be present only once. Elements in a set are not ordered.
- An *OrderedSet* is a set whose elements are ordered.
- A *Bag* is a collection that may contain duplicate elements; that is, the same instance may occur in a bag more than once. A bag is typically the result of combining navigations. This concept is introduced in Section 2.4.2 and explained further in Section 8.2. Elements in a bag are not ordered.
- A *Sequence* is a bag whose elements are ordered.

Note that a value of type *Sequence* or *OrderedSet* is ordered and not sorted. Each element has a sequence number, like array elements in programming languages. This does not mean that the element at a certain sequence number is in any sense less than or greater than the element before it. (See Section 9.3.3.)

In the R&L model, the following navigations in the context of *LoyaltyProgram* result in a collection:

```
self.participants        -- Set(Customer)
self.levels              -- OrderedSet(ServiceLevel)
```

9.1.1 Collection Constants

Constant sets, ordered sets, sequences, and bags can be specified by enumerating their elements. Curly brackets should surround the elements of the collection, and the elements are separated by commas. The type of the collection is written before the curly brackets, as shown in the following examples:

```
Set { 1 , 2 , 5 , 88 }
Set { 'apple' , 'orange', 'strawberry' }
OrderedSet { 'apple' , 'orange', 'strawberry', 'pear' }
Sequence { 1, 3, 45, 2, 3 }
Sequence { 'ape', 'nut' }
Bag {1 , 3 , 4, 3, 5 }
```

Because of the usefulness of a sequence of consecutive integers, there is a special way to specify them. The elements inside the curly brackets can be replaced by an interval specification, which consists of two expressions of type *Integer* separated by two dots (..). This specifies a sequence of all integers between the values of the first and second integer expression, including the values of both expressions themselves:

```
Sequence{ 1..(6 + 4) }
Sequence{ 1..10 }
-- are both identical to
Sequence{ 1, 2, 3, 4, 5, 6, 7, 8, 9, 10 }
```

9.1.2 Collection Type Expressions

Occasionally, one needs to explicitly state the type of a model element; for instance, when specifying an initial value. When the type of an element is a collection, this can be indicated using the words *Set*, *OrderedSet*, *Bag*, or *Sequence*, and the type of the elements of the collection between rounded brackets, as shown in the following examples:

```
Set(Customer)
Sequence(Set(ProgramPartners))
OrderedSet(ServiceLevel)
Bag(Burning)
```

9.1.3 Collections Operations

Numerous standard operations are defined on the collection types that manipulate collections in various ways. These operations are explained in the following sections.

All operations on collections are denoted in OCL expressions using an arrow; the operation following the arrow is applied to the collection before the arrow. This practice makes it possible for the user to define operations in the model that have the same names as the standard operations. The user-defined operation is taken when it follows a dot; the standard operation is taken when it follows an arrow.

All collection types are defined as value types; that is, the value of an instance cannot be changed. Therefore, collection operations do not change a collection, but they may result in a new collection.

The following invariant, from the R&L model, uses the standard operation *size*, and states that the number of participants in a loyalty program must be less than 10,000:

```
context LoyaltyProgram
inv: self.participants->size() < 10000
```

9.1.4 Treating Instances as Collections

Because the OCL syntax for applying collection operations is different from that for user-defined type operations, you can use a single instance as a collection. This collection is considered to be a set with the instance as the only element. For example, in the R&L model from Figure 2-1, the following constraint results in the value of the user-defined operation *isEmpty()* of an instance of *LoyaltyAccount:*

```
context Membership
inv: account.isEmpty()
```

Conversely, the following constraint results in the value of the *Set* operation *isEmpty,* where the *account* is used as a collection:

```
context Membership
inv: account->isEmpty()
```

This expression evaluates to true if the link from the instance of *Membership* to an instance of *LoyaltyAccount* is empty; that is, the *Membership* has no attached *LoyaltyAccount.*

9.1.5 Collections of Collections

A special feature of OCL collections is that in most cases, collections are automatically *flattened*; that is, a collection does not contain collections but only simple objects. An example is given by the following two collections. The first is a collection of collections, the second is the flattened version of the first:

```
Set { Set { 1, 2 }, Set { 3, 4 }, Set { 5, 6 } }
Set { 1, 2, 3, 4, 5, 6 }
```

When a collection is inserted into another collection, the resulting collection is automatically flattened; the elements of the inserted collection are considered direct elements of the resulting collection. The reason for this approach is that collections of collections (and even deeper nested collections) are conceptually difficult to grasp, and are not often used in practice.

For those who do want to use nested collections, there is a way to maintain the layered structure when inserting a collection into a collection. The *collectNested* operation leaves the structure intact (see Sections 9.3.10 to 9.3.12 for more information). The following sections describe the collection operations.

9.2 OPERATIONS ON COLLECTION TYPES

All collection types have the operations shown in Table 9-1 in common. These operations are defined by the abstract supertype *Collection*. Following are examples of the use of the *includes* and *includesAll* operations. In the invariant, you specify that the actual service level of a membership must be one of the service levels of the program to which the membership belongs:

```
context Membership
inv: programs.levels->includes(currentLevel)
```

The following invariant specifies that the available services for a service level must be offered by a partner of the loyalty program to which the service level belongs:

```
context ServiceLevel
inv: program.partners
            ->includesAll(self.availableServices.partner)
```

9.2.1 Operations with Variant Meaning

Some operations are defined for all collection types but have a slightly different, specialized meaning when applied to one type or another. Table 9-2 shows an overview of the operations with variant meaning defined on the four collection

Table 9-1 *Standard operations on all collection types*

Operation	Description
count(object)	The number of occurrences of the object in the collection
excludes(object)	True if the object is not an element of the collection
excludesAll(collection)	True if all elements of the parameter collection are not present in the current collection
includes(object)	True if the object is an element of the collection
includesAll(collection)	True if all elements of the parameter collection are present in the current collection
isEmpty()	True if the collection contains no elements
notEmpty()	True if the collection contains one or more elements
size()	The number of elements in the collection
sum()	The addition of all elements in the collection. The elements must be of a type supporting addition (such as *Real* or *Integer*).

types. An X mark indicates that the operation is defined for the given type; a hyphen (-) mark indicates that the operation is not defined for that type.

The *equals* and *notEquals* Operations

The *equals* operator (denoted by =) evaluates to true if all elements in two collections are the same. For sets, this means that all elements present in the first set must be present in the second set and vice versa. For ordered sets, an extra restriction specifies that the order in which the elements appear must also be the same. For two bags to be equal, not only must all elements be present in both, but the number of times an element is present must also be the same. For two sequences, the rules for bags apply, plus the extra restriction that the order of elements must be equal.

The *notEquals* operator (denoted by <>) evaluates to true if all elements in two collections are not the same. The opposite rules as for the *equals* operator apply. Both operations use the infix notation.

Table 9-2 *Collection operations with variant meaning*

Operation	Set	OrderedSet	Bag	Sequence
=	X	X	X	X
<>	X	X	X	X
-	X	X	-	-
append(object)	-	X	-	X
asBag()	X	X	X	X
asOrderedSet()	X	X	X	X
asSequence()	X	X	X	X
asSet()	X	X	X	X
at(index)	-	X	-	X
excluding(object)	X	X	X	X
first()	-	X	-	X
flatten()	X	X	X	X
including(object)	X	X	X	X
indexOf(object)	-	X	-	X
insertAt(index, object)	-	X	-	X
intersection(coll)	X	-	X	-
last()	-	X	-	X
prepend(object)	-	X	-	X
subOrderedSet(lower, upper)	-	X	-	-
subSequence(lower, upper)	-	-	-	X
symmetricDifference(coll)	X	-	-	-
union(coll)	X	X	X	X

The *including* and *excluding* Operations

The *including* operation results in a new collection with one element added to the original collection. For a bag, this description is completely true. If the collection is a set or ordered set, then the element is added only if it is not already present in the set; otherwise, the result is equal to the original collection. If the collection is a sequence or an ordered set, the element is added after all elements in the original collection.

The *excluding* operation results in a new collection with an element removed from the original collection. From a set or ordered set, it removes only one element. From a bag or sequence, it removes all occurrences of the given object.

The *flatten* Operation

The *flatten* operation changes a collection of collections into a collection of single objects. When applied to a bag, the result is also a bag. This means that when a certain object is in more than one subcollection, that object will be included in the resulting bag more than once. When applied to a set, the result is also a set. Thus, when the object is in more than one subcollection, it is included in the result only once. For example, if the original collection is the one in the first line in the following example, then the result of the *flatten* operation would be the collection in the second line.

```
Set { Set { 1, 2 }, Set { 2, 3 }, Set { 4, 5, 6 } }
Set { 1, 2, 3, 4, 5, 6 }
```

The result of the *flatten* operation executed on a bag instead of a set, is shown in the following example:

```
Bag { Set { 1, 2 }, Set { 1, 2 }, Set { 4, 5, 6 } }
Bag { 1, 1, 2, 2, 4, 5, 6 }
```

When the *flatten* operation is applied to a sequence or ordered set, the result is a sequence or ordered set (respectively). However, when the subcollections are either bags or sets, the order of the elements cannot be determined precisely. In that case, the only thing that can be assured is that the elements in a subset that comes before another subset in the original also come before the elements of the second subset in the result. For example, if the original sequence is the one in the first line of the following example, then one of the possible results of the *flatten* operation could be the one in the second line:

```
Sequence { Set { 1, 2 }, Set { 2, 3 }, Set { 4, 5, 6 } }
Sequence { 2, 1, 2, 3, 5, 6, 4 }
```

The elements of the subsets are randomly placed in the resulting sequence. There is no garantee that a second application of the flatten operation to the same sequence of sets will have the same result. Note that the *flatten* operation is defined as a recursive operation, therefore, its result is always a collection of values of one of the basic types or one of the user-defined types.

The *asSet*, *asSequence*, *asBag*, and *asOrderedSet* Operations

Instances of all four concrete collection types can be transformed into instances of another concrete collection type. This can be done using one of the *asSet*, *asSequence*, *asBag*, or *asOrderedSet* operations. Applying *asSet* on a bag or *asOrderedSet* on a sequence means that of any duplicate elements, only one remains in the result. Applying *asBag* on a sequence or *asSet* on an ordered set means that the ordering is lost. Applying *asOrderedSet* or *asSequence* on a set or bag means that the elements are placed randomly in some order in the result. Applying the operation on the same original twice does not guarantee that both results will be equal.

The *union* Operation

The *union* operation combines two collections into a new one. The union of a set with a set will result in a set; any duplicate elements are added to the result only once. Combining a set with a bag (and vice versa) results in a bag. A sequence or ordered set may not be combined with either a set or a bag, only with another ordered collection. In the result, all elements of the collection on which the operation is called go before the elements of the parameter collection.

The *intersection* Operation

The *intersection* operation results in another collection containing the elements in both collections. This operation is valid for combinations of two sets, a set and a bag, or two bags, but not for combinations involving a sequence or ordered set.

The *minus* Operation

The *minus* operation (denoted by -) results in a new set containing all the elements in the set on which the operation is called, but not in the parameter set. This operation is defined for sets and ordered sets. When applied to an ordered set, the ordering remains. The minus operation uses an infix notation. Here are some examples:

```
Set{1,4,7,10} - Set{4,7} = Set{1,10}
OrderedSet{12,9,6,3} - Set{1,3,2} = OrderedSet{12,9,6}
```

The *symmetricDifference* Operation

The *symmetricDifference* operation results in a set containing all elements in the set on which the operation is called, or in the parameter set, but not in both. This operation is defined on sets only. Here is an example:

```
Set{1,4,7,10}.symmetricDifference(Set{4,5,7}) = Set{1,5,10}
```

9.2.2 Operations on *OrderedSets* and *Sequences* Only

All the operations defined only for the *OrderedSet* and *Sequence* types involve the ordering of the elements. There are nine such operations:

- The *first* and *last* operations result in the first and the last elements of the collection, respectively.
- The *at* operation results in the element at the given position.
- The *indexOf* operation results in an integer value that indicates the position of the element in the collection. When the element is present more than once in the collection, the result is the position of the first element. Note that the index numbers start with one, not zero, as is often the case in programming languages.
- The *insertAt* operation results in a sequence or ordered set that has an extra element inserted at the given position.
- The *subSequence* operation may be applied to sequences only, and results in a sequence that contains the elements from the lower index to the upper index, inclusive, in the original order.
- The *subOrderedSet* operation may be applied to ordered sets only. Its result is equal to the *subSequence* operation, although it results in an ordered set instead of a sequence.
- The *append* and *prepend* operations add an element to a sequence as the last or first element, respectively.

Here are some examples:

```
Sequence{'a','b','c','c','d','e'}->first() = 'a'
OrderedSet{'a','b','c','d'}->last() = 'd'
Sequence{'a','b','c','c','d','e'}->at( 3 ) = 'c'
Sequence{'a','b','c','c','d','e'}->indexOf( 'c' ) = 3
OrderedSet{'a','b','c','d'}->insertAt( 3, 'X' ) =
                              OrderedSet{'a','b','X','c','d'}
Sequence{'a','b','c','c','d','e'}->subSequence( 3, 5 ) =
                                   Sequence{'c','c','d'}
OrderedSet{'a','b','c','d'}->subOrderedSet( 2, 3 ) =
                                   OrderedSet{'b','c'}
Sequence{'a','b','c','c','d','e'}->append( 'X' ) =
                         Sequence{'a','b','c','c','d','e','X'}
```

```
Sequence{'a','b','c','c','d','e'}->prepend( 'X' ) =
                        Sequence{'X','a','b','c','c','d','e'}
```

9.3 LOOP OPERATIONS OR ITERATORS

A number of standard OCL operations enable you to loop over the elements in a collection. These operations take each element in the collection and evaluate an expression on it. Loop operations are also called *iterators* or *iterator operations*. Every loop operation has an OCL expression as parameter. This is called the *body*, or *body parameter*, of the operation. The following sections explain each of the loop operations in more detail. Table 9-3 shows an overview of the loop operations defined on the four collection types.

9.3.1 Iterator Variables

Every iterator operation may have an extra (optional) parameter, an *iterator variable*. An iterator variable is a variable that is used within the body parameter to indicate the element of the collection for which the body parameter is being calculated. The type of this iterator variable is always the type of the elements in the collection. Because the type is known, it may be omitted in the declaration of the iterator variable. Thus, the next two examples are both correct. The following invariants state that the number of the loyalty account must be unique within a loyalty program:

```
context LoyaltyProgram
inv: self.Membership.account->isUnique( acc | acc.number )

context LoyaltyProgram
inv: self.Membership.account->isUnique( acc: LoyaltyAccount
                                        | acc.number )
```

It is recommended to use iterator variables when the type of the elements in the collection has features with the same names as the contextual instance. For example, if the class *LoyaltyProgram* itself has an attribute *number*, then leaving out the iterator variable seems to render the preceding constraints ambiguous. Is the *number* parameter refering to the number of the loyalty program or to the number of the loyalty account? Although the OCL specification clearly defines the meaning of the constraint, the human reader will be guided by the use of iterator variables.

The OCL specification states that in a loop expression, namespaces are nested. The innermost namespace is that of the type of the elements of the collection; in this case, *LoyaltyAccount*. When a name in the body parameter cannot be found in

Table 9-3 *Loop operations on all collection types*

Operation	Description
any(expr)	Returns a random element of the source collection for which the expression *expr* is true
collect(expr)	Returns the collection of objects that result from evaluating *expr* for each element in the source collection
collectNested(expr)	Returns a collection of collections that result from evaluating *expr* for each element in the source collection
exists(expr)	Returns true if there is at least one element in the source collection for which *expr* is true
forAll(expr)	Returns true if *expr* is true for all elements in the source collection
isUnique(expr)	Returns true if *expr* has a unique value for all elements in the source collection
iterate(...)	Iterates over all elements in the source collection
one(expr)	Returns true if there is exactly one element in the source collection for which *expr* is true
reject(expr)	Returns a subcollection of the source collection containing all elements for which *expr* is false
select(expr)	Returns a subcollection of the source collection containing all elements for which *expr* is false
sortedBy(expr)	Returns a collection containing all elements of the source collection ordered by *expr*

the innermost namespace, it will be searched in other namespaces. First, the namespaces of any enclosing loop expressions will be searched. Next, the namespace of the contextual instance will be searched. Thus, the following invariant is still a correct representation of the intended meaning:

```
context LoyaltyProgram
inv: self.Membership.account->isUnique( number )
```

When the body parameter should refer to the feature of the contextual instance, it should be prefixed *self*. In the preceding example, this results in a rather pointless, but correct invariant. For every account in the program, the number of the program itself will be tested. This number will be the same for every element of the collection; therefore, the expression will always have *false* as result:

```
context LoyaltyProgram
inv: self.Membership.account->isUnique( self.number )
```

The iterator variable cannot be omitted in all circumstances. It can be omitted only if an explicit reference to the iterator is not needed in the expression. For example, the following expression cannot be rewritten without use of an iterator variable because of the reference to the iterator:

```
context ProgramPartner
inv: self.programs.partners->
                    select(p : ProgramPartner | p <> self)
```

This expression results in the collection of all program partners that are in the same loyalty programs as the context program partner.

9.3.2 The *isUnique* Operation

Quite often in a collection of elements, we want a certain aspect of the elements to be unique for each element in the collection. For instance, in a collection of employees of a company, the employee number must be unique. To state this fact, we can use the *isUnique* operation. The parameter of this operation is usually a feature of the type of the elements in the collection. The result is either true or false. The operation will loop over all elements and compare the values by calculating the parameter expression for all elements. If none of the values is equal to another, the result is true; otherwise, the result is false. An example was given in Section 9.3.1.

9.3.3 The *sortedBy* Operation

In Section 9.1, we mentioned that both *Sequence* or *OrderedSet* instances are ordered and not sorted. We can demand an ordering on the elements of any collection using the *sortedBy* operation. The parameter of this operation is a property of the type of the elements in the collection. For this property, the *lesserThan* operation (denoted by <) must be defined. The result is a sequence or ordered set, depending on the type of the original collection. Applying this operation to a sequence will result in a sequence; applying this operation to an ordered set will result in an ordered set.

The operation will loop over all elements in the original collection and will order all elements according to the value derived from calculating the parameter property. The first element in the result is the element for which the property is the lowest.

Again, we take as an example the number of the *LoyaltyAccount* in the R&L system. The following defines an attribute *sortedAccounts* that holds all loyalty accounts of a loyalty program sorted by number:

```
context LoyaltyProgram
def: sortedAccounts : Sequence(LoyaltyAccount) =
                    self.Membership.account->sortedBy( number )
```

9.3.4 The *select* Operation

Sometimes an expression using operations and navigations results in a collection, but we are interested only in a special subset of the collection. The *select* operation enables us to specify a selection from the original collection. The result of the *select* operation is always a proper subset of the original collection.

The parameter of the *select* operation is a boolean expression that specifies which elements we want to select from the collection. The result of *select* is the collection that contains all elements for which the boolean expression is true. The following expression selects all transactions on a *CustomerCard* that have more than 100 *points*:

```
context CustomerCard
inv: self.transactions->select( points > 100 )->notEmpty()
```

We can explain the meaning of the *select* operation in an operational way, but *select* is still an operation without side effects; it results in a new set. The result of *select* can be described by the following pseudocode:

```
element = collection.firstElement();
while( collection.notEmpty() ) do
    if( <expression-with-element> )
    then
        result.add(element);
    endif
    element = collection.nextElement();
endwhile
return result;
```

9.3.5 The *reject* Operation

The *reject* operation is analogous to *select*, with the distinction that *reject* selects all elements from the collection for which the expression evaluates to false. The existence of *reject* is merely a convenience. The following two invariants are semantically equivalent:

```
context Customer
inv: Membership.account->select( points > 0 )
```

```
context Customer
inv: Membership.account->reject( not (points > 0) )
```

9.3.6 The *any* Operation

To obtain any element from a collection for which a certain condition holds, we can use the *any* operation. The body parameter of this operation is a boolean expression. The result is a single element of the original collection. The operation will loop over all elements in the original collection and find one element that upholds the condition specified by the body parameter. If the condition holds for more than one element, one of them is randomly chosen. If the condition does not hold for any element in the source collection, the result is undefined (see Section 10.6).

Again, we take as example the number of the *LoyaltyAccount* in the R&L system. The following expression from the context of *LoyaltyProgram* results in a loyalty account randomly picked from the set of accounts in the program that have a number lower than 10,000:

```
self.Membership.account->any( number < 10000 )
```

9.3.7 The *forAll* Operation

We often want to specify that a certain condition must hold for all elements of a collection. The *forAll* operation on collections can be used for this purpose. The result of the *forAll* operation is a boolean value. It is true if the expression is true for all elements of the collection. If the expression is false for one or more elements in the collection, then *forAll* results in false. For example, consider the following expression:

```
context LoyaltyProgram
inv: participants->forAll( age() <= 70 )
```

This expression evaluates to true if the age of all participants in a loyalty program is less than or equal to 70. If the age of at least one (or more) customers exceeds 70, the result is false.

The *forAll* operation has an extended variant in which multiple iterator variables can be declared. All iterator variables iterate over the complete collection. Effectively, this is a short notation for a nested *forAll* expression on the collection.

The next example, which is a complex way to express the *isUnique* operation, shows the use of multiple iterator variables:

```
context LoyaltyProgram
inv: self.participants->forAll(c1, c2 |
                    c1 <> c2 implies c1.name <> c2.name)
```

This expression evaluates to true if the names of all customers of a loyalty program are different. It is semantically equivalent to the following expression, which uses nested *forAll* operations:

```
context LoyaltyProgram
inv: self.participants->forAll( c1 |
            self.participants->forAll( c2 |
                    c1 <> c2 implies c1.name <> c2.name ))
```

Although the number of iterators is unrestricted, more than two iterators are seldom used. The multiple iterators are allowed only with the *forAll* operation and not with any other operation that uses iterators.

9.3.8 The *exists* Operation

Often, we want to specify that there is at least one object in a collection for which a certain condition holds. The *exists* operation on collections can be used for this purpose. The result of the *exists* operation is a boolean. It is true if the expression is true for at least one element of the collection. If the expression is false for all elements in the collection, then the *exists* operation results in false. For example, in the context of a *LoyaltyAccount,* we can state that if the attribute *points* is greater than zero, there exists a *Transaction* with *points* greater than zero.

```
context LoyaltyAccount
inv: points > 0 implies transactions->exists(t | t.points > 0)
```

Obviously, there is a relationship between the *exists* and the *forAll* operations. The following two expressions are equivalent:

```
collection->exists( <expression> )
not collection->forAll( not < expression> )
```

9.3.9 The *one* Operation

The *one* operation gives a boolean result stating whether there is exactly one element in the collection for which a condition holds. The body parameter of this operation, stating the condition, is a boolean expression. The operation will loop over all elements in the original collection and find all elements for which the condition holds. If there is exactly one such element, then the result is true; otherwise, the result is false.

Again, we take as an example the number attribute of the *LoyaltyAccount* class in the R&L system. The following invariant states that there may be only one loyalty account that has a number lower than 10,000:

```
context LoyaltyProgram
inv: self.Membership.account->one( number < 10000 )
```

Note the difference between the *any* and *one* operations. The *any* operation can be seen as a variant of the *select* operation: its result is an element selected from the source collection. The *one* operation is a variant of the *exists* operation: its result is either true or false depending on whether or not a certain element exists in the source collection.

9.3.10 The *collect* Operation

The *collect* operation iterates over the collection, computes a value for each element of the collection, and gathers the evaluated values into a new collection. The type of the elements in the resulting collection is usually different from the type of the elements in the collection on which the operation is applied. The following expression from the context of *LoyaltyAccount* represents a collection of integer values that holds the values of the *point* attribute in all linked *Transaction* instances:

```
transactions->collect( points )
```

You can use this expression to state an invariant on this collection of integer values. For example, you could demand that at least one of the values be 500:

```
context LoyaltyAccount
inv: transactions->collect( points )->
                    exists( p : Integer | p = 500 )
```

The result of the *collect* operation on a set or bag is a bag and on an ordered set or sequence, the result is a sequence. The result of the *collect* is always a flattened collection (see Section 9.1.5).

9.3.11 Shorthand Notation for *collect*

Because the *collect* operation is used extensively, a shorthand notation has been introduced. This shorthand can be used only when there can be no misinterpretations. Instead of the preceding constraint, we can write

```
context LoyaltyAccount
inv: transactions.points->exists(p : Integer | p = 500 )
```

In this expression, *transactions* is a set of *Transactions*; therefore, only the set properties can be used on it. The notation *transactions.points* is shorthand for *transactions->collect(points)*. Thus, when we take a property of a collection using a dot, this is interpreted as applying the *collect* operation, where the property is used as the body parameter.

9.3.12 The *collectNested* Operation

The *collectNested* operation iterates over the collection, like the *collect* operation. Whereas the result of the *collect* is always a flattened collection (see Section 9.1.5), the result of the *collectNested* operation maintains the nested structure of collections within collections. The following expression from the context of *Customer* represents a collection of collections of *Service* instances. In fact, the type of this expression is *Bag(Set(Service))*:

```
self.programs->collect(partners)->
                              collectNested( deliveredServices )
```

9.3.13 The *iterate* Operation

The *iterate* operation is the most fundamental and complex of the loop operations. At the same time, it is the most generic loop operation. All other loop operations can be described as a special case of *iterate*. The syntax of the *iterate* operation is as follows:

```
collection->iterate( element : Type1;
                     result  : Type2 = <expression>
                   | <expression-with-element-and-result>)
```

The variable *element* is the iterator variable. The resulting value is accumulated in the variable *result*, which is also called the *accumulator*. The accumulator gets an initial value, given by the expression after the equal sign. None of the parameters is optional.

The result of the *iterate* operation is a value obtained by iterating over all elements in a collection. For each successive element in the source collection, the body expression (*<expression-with-element-and-result>*) is calculated using the previous value of the *result* variable. A simple example of the iterate operation is given by the following expression, which results in the sum of the elements of a set of integers:

```
Set{1,2,3}->iterate( i: Integer, sum: Integer = 0 | sum + i )
```

In this case, we could have simplified the constraint by using the *sum* operation defined on *Integer*. The *sum* operation is a shortcut for the specific use of the *iterate* operation.

A more complex example of the *iterate* operation can be found in the R&L model. Suppose that the class *ProgramPartner* needs a query operation that returns all transactions on services of all partners that burn points. It can be defined as follows:

```
context ProgramPartner
def: getBurningTransactions(): Set(Transaction) =
    self.deliveredServices.transactions->iterate(
        t          : Transaction;
        resultSet : Set(Transaction) = Set{} |
        if t.oclIsTypeOf( Burning ) then
            resultSet.including( t )
        else
            resultSet
        endif
    )
```

First, a bag of transactions is obtained by collecting the transactions of all services of this partner. For every successive transaction in the bag, the *if* expression is evaluated. At the start, *resultSet* is empty, but when a burning transaction is encountered, it is added to *resultSet*. If the current element is not a burning transaction, the result of the evaluation of this element is an unchanged *resultSet*. This value will be used in the evaluation of the next element of the source collection.

Chapter 10

Advanced Constructs

This chapter describes all the constructs with which you can write more advanced expressions, ranging from expressions that can be used only in postconditions to definitions of variables that are local to a context definition.

10.1 CONSTRUCTS FOR POSTCONDITIONS

There are two ways to write constraints for operations: preconditions and post-conditions. In postconditions, you can use a number of special constructs. Two special keywords represent, to some extent, the working of time: *result* and *@pre*. Another aspect of time is represented by messaging. The following subsections explain all the constructs that can be used in postconditions only.

10.1.1 The *@pre* Keyword

The *@pre* keyword indicates the value of an attribute or association at the start of the execution of the operation. The keyword must be postfixed to the name of the item concerned. In the case of an operation, it must proceed the parentheses, as shown in the following example:

```
context LoyaltyProgram::enroll(c : Customer)
pre : not (participants->includes(c))
post: participants = participants@pre->including(c)
```

The precondition of this example states that the customer to be enrolled cannot already be a member of the program. The postcondition states that the set of customers after the enroll operation must be the set of customers before the operation with the enrolled customer added to it. We could also add a second postcondition stating that the membership for the new customer has a loyalty account with zero points and no transactions:

```
post: Membership->select(m : Membership | m.participants = c)->
         forAll( account->notEmpty() and
                 account.points = 0  and
                 account.transactions->isEmpty() )
```

10.1.2 The *result* Keyword

The keyword *result* indicates the return value from the operation. The type of *result* is defined by the return type of the operation. In the following example, the type of *result* is *LoyaltyProgram*. Note that a navigation from an association class—in this case, *Membership*—always results in a single object (see Section 8.2.1):

```
context Transaction::getProgram() : LoyaltyProgram
post: result = self.card.Membership.programs
```

In this example, the result of the *getProgram* operation is the loyalty program against which the transaction was made.

10.1.3 The *oclIsNew* Operation

To determine whether an object is created during the execution of an operation, the *oclIsNew* operation can be used. It returns true if the object to which it is applied did not exist at precondition time, but does exist at postcondition time. In the following example, the postcondition states that in between pre- and postcondition time, at least one customer has been added to the set of participants. This customer object is created between pre- and postcondition time, its name is equal to the parameter *n*, and its date of birth is equal to the parameter *d*:

```
context LoyaltyProgram::enrollAndCreateCustomer( n : String,
                                                 d: Date ) : Customer
pre : -- none
post: result.oclIsNew() and
      result.name = n and
      result.dateOfBirth = d and
      participants->includes( result )
```

Note that a postcondition does not specify the statements in the body of the operation. There are many ways in which the postcondition can become true.

10.1.4 The *isSent* Operator

To specify that communication has taken place, the *isSent* operator (denoted as ^) may be used in postconditions. This operator takes a target object and a message as operands. It has a boolean result. The following example on the standard observer pattern states that the message *update(12, 14)* has been sent to the target object *observer* between pre- and postcondition time of the *hasChanged* operation:

```
context Subject::hasChanged()
post:  observer^update(12, 14)
```

As with messages in an interaction diagram, *update* is either a call to an operation defined in the type of *observer*, or it is the sending of a signal specified in the UML model. The argument(s) of the message expression (12 and 14 in this example) must conform to the parameters of the operation or signal definition.

If the actual arguments of the operation or signal are not known, or not restricted in any way, they can be left unspecified. This is indicated by a question mark. Following the question mark is an optional type, which may be necessary to find the correct operation when the same operation exists with different parameter types, as shown in the following example:

```
context Subject::hasChanged()
post:  observer^update(? : Integer, ? : Integer)
```

This example states that the message *update* has been sent to *observer*, but that the actual values of the parameters are not known or not relevant.

Note that the postcondition does not state that the message has been received by the target. Depending on the communication mechanism between source and target, some messages may get lost or be delivered later than postcondition time.

10.1.5 The *message* Operator

During execution of an operation many messages may have been sent that represent calls to the same operation, or send signals according to the same signal definition. To work with collections of messages, OCL defines a special *OclMessage* type. Any operation call or signal being sent is virtually wrapped in an instance of *OclMessage*. One can obtain access to all *OclMessages* that wrap a matching call or signal, through the *message operator* (denoted as ^^). A call or signal matches when the operation name and the argument types given after the message operator correspond to the formal definition of the operation or signal, as shown in the following example:

```
observer^^update(12, 14)
```

This expression results in the sequence of messages sent that match *update(12, 14)* being sent by the contextual instance to the object called *observer* during the execution of the operation. Each element of the sequence is an instance of *OclMessage*. Any collection operation can subsequently be applied to this sequence.

Because the message operator results in a sequence of instances of *OclMessage*, it can also be used to specify collections of messages sent to different targets, as shown in the following example:

```
context Subject::hasChanged()
post:  let messages : Sequence(OclMessage) =
              observers->collect(o |
                          o^^update(? : Integer, ? : Integer) )
       in messages->notEmpty()
```

The local variable *messages* is a sequence of *OclMessage* instances built from the messages that have been sent to one of the *observers* and match *update(? : Integer, ? : Integer)* as well. Note that the *collect* operation flattens the sequence, so that its elements are of type *OclMessage*, and not of type *Sequence(OclMessage)*.

The message operator helps explain the *isSent* operator in another way. Virtually, the *isSent* operator represents the application of the operation *notEmpty* on the sequence of *OclMessages*. Therefore, the following postcondition is semantically equal to the postcondition in Section 10.1.4:

```
context Subject::hasChanged()
post:  observer^^update(12, 14)->notEmpty()
```

In a postcondition with a message operand, one can refer to the parameters of the operation or signal using the formal parameter names from the operation or signal definition. For example, if the operation *update* has been defined with formal parameters named *i* and *j*, we can write the following:

```
context Subject::hasChanged()
post: let messages : Sequence(OclMessage) =
                      observer^^update(? : Integer, ? : Integer) in
      messages->notEmpty() and
      messages->exists( m | m.i > 0 and m.j >= m.i )
```

In this example, the values of the parameters *i* and *j* are not known, but some restrictions apply. First, *i* must be greater than zero; and second, the value of parameter *j* must be larger than or equal to *i*.

10.2 OPERATIONS OF THE *OCLMESSAGE* TYPE

The *OclMessage* type, as explained in Section 10.1.5, has a number of operations. The operations defined for the *OclMessage* type are shown in Table 10-1.

10.2.1 The *hasReturned* and *result* Operations

Some messages have result values. A message representing a signal sent is by definition asynchronous, so there never is a return value. If there is a logical return value, it must be modeled as a separate signal message. However, an operation call has a potential return value, indicated by the return type in its signature.

Table 10-1 *Message related operations on any OCL instance*

Expression	Result Type
isSignalSent()	Boolean
isOperationCall()	Boolean
hasReturned()	Boolean
result()	Return type of called operation

In a postcondition, the return value of an operation call is accessible from an *OclMessage* instance. It is available only if the operation has already returned upon postcondition time. This is not always the case, because operation calls may be asynchronous.

Therefore, the *OclMessage* type has two operations: *hasReturned* and *result*. The *hasReturned* operation results in true if the operation call wrapped in the *OclMessage* instance has already finished executing and has returned a value. The *result* operation results in the return value of the called operation. For instance, in the model from Figure 10-1, if *getMoney* is an operation on class *Company* that returns a boolean, as in *Company::getMoney(amount : Integer) : Boolean*, we can write

```
context Person::giveSalary(amount : Integer)
post: let message : OclMessage =
                    company^^getMoney(amount)->any( true )
      in message.hasReturned() and
         message.result() = true
```

If the *hasReturned* operation results in false, then the *result* operation will return undefined (see Section 10.6).

10.2.2 The *isSignalCall* and *isOperationCall* operations

Two other operations are defined on the *OclMessage* type. The *isSignalCall* and *isOperationCall* operations can be used to determine whether a message corresponds to an operation or to a signal. Both have a boolean result, and no parameters.

10.3 PACKAGING EXPRESSIONS

Like every other model element, OCL expressions may be included in a package. In general, the model element that is the context of an OCL expression is the owner of that expression, and the expression will be part of the same package as its context. When the expression is present in a diagram, it is obvious that the package that owns the expression is the package that owns its context. Because expressions are often written separate from the diagrams, it is not always clear to which package they belong.

To specify explicitly the package in which an OCL expression belongs, you have two options. The context definition may contain a pathname indicating the package to which the context belongs, or the context definition may be enclosed between *package* and *endpackage* statements. These statements have the following syntax, where the boldface words are keywords:

```
package Package::SubPackage

context X
inv: ... some invariant ...

context X::operationName(..)
pre: ... some precondition ...

endpackage
```

The preceding example has the same meaning as the following two expressions:

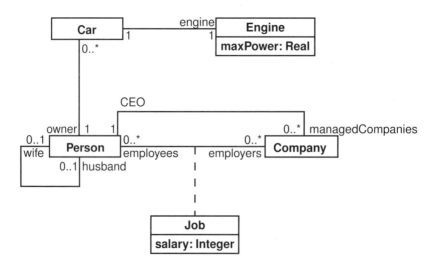

Figure 10-1 Persons *working for* Companies, *extended*

```
context Package::SubPackage::X
inv: ... some invariant ...

context Package::SubPackage::X::operationName(..)
pre: ... some precondition ...
```

An OCL file (or stream) may contain any number of package statements and any number of expressions enclosed in context definitions, thus allowing all invariants, preconditions, and postconditions to be written and stored in one file. This file may coexist with a UML model containing the diagrams as a separate entity.

10.4 LOCAL VARIABLES

Sometimes a sub-expression is used more than once in an expression. A so-called *let* expression enables you to define a local variable to represent the value of the sub-expression. The variable must be declared with a name, a type, and an expression that specifies its value. The variable may be used only in the expression following the keyword *in*. A *let* expression may be included in any OCL expression. The following example uses the model shown in Figure 10-1:

```
context Person
inv: let income : Integer = self.job.salary->sum()
     in
       if isUnemployed then
          income < 100
       else
          income >= 100
       endif
```

Let expressions may be nested, but a more convenient manner of defining a number of local variables is to include them in one *let* expression. In that case, they must be separated by a comma:

```
context Person
inv: let income : Integer = self.job.salary->sum(),
         carSize : Real = self.car.engine.maxPower
     in
       if isUnemployed then
          income < 100 and carSize < 1.0
       else
          income >= 100  and carSize >= 1.0
       endif
```

10.5 TUPLES AND TUPLE TYPES

It is possible to compose several values into a *tuple*. A tuple consists of named parts, each of which can have a distinct type. Each tuple is a value itself. As OCL is a strongly typed language, each tuple has its own type. These tuple types do not have a name. They are either implicitly defined by a certain tuple value, or explicitly, but namelessly, defined; for instance, in the type expression of a local variable. Some examples of tuple values, and the way to write them, are:

```
Tuple {name: String = 'John',  age: Integer = 10}
Tuple {a: Collection(Integer) = Set{1, 3, 4},
       b: String = 'foo',
       c: String = 'bar'}
```

The parts of a tuple are enclosed in curly brackets, and separated by commas. The type names are optional, and the order of the parts is unimportant. Thus, the following three expressions indicate the same tuple:

```
Tuple {name: String = 'John', age: Integer = 10}
Tuple {name = 'John', age = 10}
Tuple {age = 10, name = 'John'}
```

Some examples of tuple types, and the way to write them, are:

```
TupleType(name: String, age: Integer)
TupleType(a: Collection(Integer),
          b: String,
          c: String)
```

Here, the parts of the tuple are enclosed in parentheses, again separated by commas. The type names are mandatory, but the order of the parts is still unimportant. In a tuple value, the values of the parts may be indicated by arbitrary OCL expressions; for example, in the model from Figure 10-1, we may write

```
context Person
def: statistics : Set(TupleType(company: Company,
                                numEmployees: Integer,
                                wellpaidEmployees: Set(Person),
                                totalSalary: Integer)) =
      managedCompanies->collect(c |
        Tuple { company: Company = c,
                numEmployees: Integer = c.employees->size(),
                wellpaidEmployees: Set(Person) =
                  c.Job->select(salary>10000).employees->asSet(),
                totalSalary: Integer = c.Job.salary->sum()
              }
      )
```

The preceding expression results in a bag of tuples summarizing the company, the number of employees, the best-paid employees, and the total salary costs of each company a person manages.

The parts of a tuple are accessed by their names, using the same dot notation that is used for accessing attributes. Thus, the following two statements are true, if somewhat pointless:

```
Tuple {x: Integer = 5, y: String = 'hi'}.x = 5
Tuple {x: Integer = 5, y: String = 'hi'}.y = 'hi'
```

A more meaningful example, using the definition of *statistics* above, is:

```
context Company::isTopManager( p: Person ) : Boolean
body: p.statistics->sortedBy(totalSalary)
                 ->last().company = self
```

The operation *isTopManager* is a query operation that returns true if the given person manages the contextual instance and he or she manages a set of employees that together command the highest total salary. In this expression, both *totalSalary* and *company* are accessing tuple parts.

10.6 UNDEFINED VALUES, THE *OCLVOID* TYPE

Some expressions will, when evaluated, have an undefined value. For instance, typecasting with the *oclAsType* operation to a type that the object does not support, or getting an element from an empty collection, will result in an undefined value.

The undefined value is the only instance of the type *OclVoid*. The *OclVoid* type conforms to all types in the system. There is an explicit operation for testing if the value of an expression is undefined. The operation *oclIsUndefined* is an operation on *OclAny* (see Section 10.10) that results in true if its argument is undefined, and false otherwise.

In general, an expression for which one of the parts is undefined will itself be undefined. Note some important exceptions to this rule, however. First, there are the logical operators:

- True or undefined = True
- False and undefined = False
- False implies undefined = True

The rules for *or* and *and* are valid irrespective of the order of the arguments and irrespective of whether the value of the other sub-expression is known or not. The *if* expression is another exception. It will be valid as long as the chosen branch is valid, irrespective of the value of the other branch.

10.7 RETYPING OR CASTING

In some circumstances, it is desirable to use a feature that is defined on a subtype of the type that is expected at that point in the expression. Because the feature is not defined on the expected type, this results in a type conformance error.

When you are certain that the actual type of the object is the subtype, the object can be retyped using the operation *oclAsType*, which takes as parameter a type name. This operation results in the same object, but the expected type within the expression is the indicated parameter. When you have an object *object* of type *Type1*, and *Type2* is another type, it is allowable to write

```
object.oclAsType(Type2) --- evaluates to object with type Type2
```

An object can only be re-typed to one of its subtypes; therefore, in the example, *Type2* must be a subtype of *Type1*.

If the actual type of the object is not a subtype of the type to which it is re-typed, the result of the expression is undefined (see Section 10.6).

10.8 TYPE CONFORMANCE RULES

OCL is a typed language. When you are constructing a new expression from other expressions, the sub expressions and the operator must "fit." If they don't, the expression is invalid, and any parser will complain that the expression contains a type conformance error. The definition of *conformance* that is used within OCL is as follows:

> **Type1 conforms to Type2 if an instance of Type1 can be substituted at each place where an instance of Type2 is expected.**

These are the type conformance rules used in OCL expressions:

1. *Type1* conforms to *Type2* when they are identical.
2. *Type1* conforms to *Type2* when *Type1* is a subtype of *Type2*.
3. Each type is a subtype of *OclAny*.
4. Type conformance is transitive; that is, if *Type1* conforms to *Type2* and *Type2* conforms to *Type3*, then *Type1* conforms to *Type3*. Together with the first rule, this means that a type conforms to any of its predecessors in an inheritance tree.
5. *Integer* is a subtype of *Real* and therefore conforms to *Real*.
6. Every type *Collection(T)* is a subtype of *OclAny*. The types *Set(T)*, *Bag(T)*, *OrderedSet(T)*, and *Sequence(T)* are all subtypes of *Collection(T)*.
7. *Collection(Type1)* conforms to *Collection(Type2)* if *Type1* conforms to *Type2*.
8. *Set(T)* does not conform to *OrderedSet(T)*, *Bag(T)*, or *Sequence(T)*.
9. *OrderedSet(T)* does not conform to *Set(T)*, *Bag(T)*, or *Sequence(T)*.

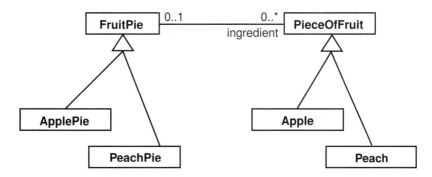

Figure 10-2 *Invariants on subtypes*

10. *Bag(T)* does not conform to *Set(T)*, *OrderedSet(T)*, or *Sequence(T)*.
11. *Sequence(T)* does not conform to *Set(T)*, *OrderedSet(T)*, or *Bag(T)*.

For example, in Figure 10-2, *PeachPie* and *ApplePie* are two separate subtypes of *FruitPie*. In this example, the following statements are true:

- *Set(ApplePie)* conforms to *Set(FruitPie)*.
- *Set(ApplePie)* conforms to *Collection(ApplePie)*.
- *Set(ApplePie)* conforms to *Collection(FruitPie)*.
- *Set(ApplePie)* does not conform to *Bag(ApplePie)*.
- *Bag(ApplePie)* does not conform to *Set(ApplePie)*.
- *Set(AppePie)* does not conform to *Set(PeachPie)*.

10.9 ACCESSING OVERRIDEN FEATURES

Whenever features are redefined within a type, the feature of the supertypes can be accessed using the *oclAsType()* operation. Whenever you have a class *B* as a subtype of class *A*, and a feature *f1* of both *A* and *B*, you can write

```
context B
inv: self.oclAsType(A).f1   -- accesses the f1 feature defined in A
inv: self.f1                -- accesses the f1 feature defined in B
```

Figure 10-3 shows an example where such a construct is needed. This model fragment contains an ambiguity in the following OCL expression on class *Dependency*:

```
context Dependency
inv: self.source <> self
```

This can mean either normal association navigation, which is inherited from *ModelElement*, or it might mean navigation through the dotted line as an association

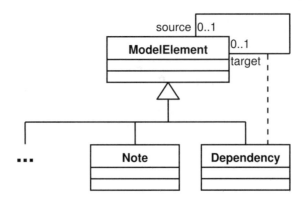

Figure 10-3 *Accessing overridden features example*

class. Both possible navigations use the same rolename, so this is always ambiguous. Using *oclAsType()*, you can distinguish between them with

```
context Dependency
inv: self.oclAsType(Dependency).source <> self
```

or

```
context Dependency
inv: self.oclAsType(ModelElement).source <> self
```

10.10 THE *OCLANY* TYPE

A number of operations are useful for every type of OCL instance. Therefore, the OCL Standard Library has a type called *OclAny*. When OCL expressions are being evaluated, the type *OclAny* is considered to be the supertype of all types in the model. All predefined types and all user-defined types inherit the features of *OclAny*.

To avoid name conflicts between features from the model and features inherited from *OclAny*, all names of the features of *OclAny* start with *ocl*. Although theoretically there may still be name conflicts, you can avoid them by not using the *ocl* prefix in your user-defined types. The operations defined for all OCL objects are shown in Table 10-2.

10.10.1 Operations on *OclAny*

The *equals* and *notEquals* operations are redefined for most types in the Ocl Standard Library, and are explained elsewhere in this book. The *oclIsNew* operation is

Table 10-2 *Operations on any OCL instance*

Expression	Result Type
object = (object2 : OclAny)	Boolean
object <> (object2 : OclAny)	Boolean
object.oclIsUndefined()	Boolean
object.oclIsKindOf(type : OclType)	Boolean
object.oclIsTypeOf(type : OclType)	Boolean
object.oclIsNew()	Boolean
object.oclInState()	Boolean
object.oclAsType(type : OclType)	type
object.oclInState(str: StateName)	Boolean
type::allInstances()	Set(type)

explained in Section 10.1.3, the *oclAsType* operation is explained in Section 10.7, and the *oclIsUndefined* operation is explained in Section 10.6. Two other operations allow access to the metalevel of your model, which can be useful for advanced modelers.

The *oclIsTypeOf* operation results in true only if the type of the object is identical to the argument. The *oclIsKindOf* operation results in true if the type of the object is identical to the argument, or identical to any of the subtypes of the argument. The following examples, which are based on Figure 10-4, show the difference between the *oclIsKindOf* and *oclIsTypeOf* operations. For a *Transaction*, the following invariants are valid:

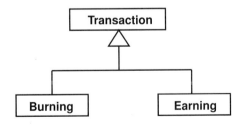

Figure 10-4 *Difference between* oclIsKindOf *and* oclIsTypeOf

```
context Transaction
inv: self.oclIsKindOf(Transaction) = true
inv: self.oclIsTypeOf(Transaction) = true
inv: self.oclIsTypeOf(Burning) = false
inv: self.oclIsKindOf(Burning) = false
```

For the subclass *Burning,* the following invariants are valid:

```
context Burning
inv: self.oclIsKindOf(Transaction) = true
inv: self.oclIsTypeOf(Transaction) = false
inv: self.oclIsTypeOf(Burning) = true
inv: self.oclIsKindOf(Burning) = true
inv: self.oclIsTypeOf(Earning) = false
inv: self.oclIsKindOf(Earning) = false
```

The *oclIsKindOf* and *oclIsTypeOf* operations are often used to specify invariants on subclasses. For example, Figure 10-2 shows a general association between *FruitPie* and *PieceOfFruit.* For the different subtypes of *FruitPie,* only specific subtypes of *PieceOfFruit* are acceptable.

Using *oclType* or one of the other operations, you can state the invariants for the subtypes of *FruitPie*: *ApplePie* and *PeachPie*:

```
context ApplePie
inv: self.ingredient->forAll(oclIsKindOf(Apple))
```

```
context PeachPie
inv: self.ingredient->forAll(oclIsKindOf(Peach))
```

The *oclInState* Operation

The *oclInState* operation is an operation that has been defined on the *OclAny* type; but in fact it is useful only for types that might have a statechart attached. It takes as a parameter a state name, and results in true if the object is in that state. For nested states, the statenames can be combined using the double colon (::). In the example statemachine shown in Figure 10-5, the statenames used can be *On, Off,*

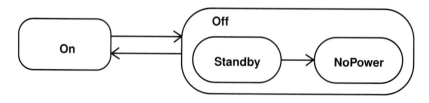

Figure 10-5 *Example statechart*

Off::Standby, Off::NoPower. If the classifier of *object* has the aforementioned associated statemachine, valid OCL expressions are as follows:

```
object.oclInState(On)
object.oclInState(Off)
object.oclInstate(Off::Standby)
object.oclInState(Off::NoPower)
```

If multiple statemachines are attached to the object's classifier, then the statename can be prefixed with the name of the statemachine containing the state and the double colon (::), as with nested states.

10.10.2 The *allInstances* Operation

The *allInstances* operation is a class operation that can be applied only to classes. In all other cases, it will result in undefined. For a class, it results in a set of all instances of that class, including all instances of its subclasses. The following expression results in the set of all instances of class *Transaction*, including all instances of type *Burning* and *Earning*:

```
Transaction::allInstances()
```

The use of *allInstances* is discouraged (see Section 3.10.3).

Glossary

Change event
An event that is generated when one or more attributes or associations change value according to an expression.

Context
The element specified in one of the UML diagrams for which the OCL expression is defined.

Context definition
The text or symbol that defines the relationship between an OCL expression and the element in the part of the model that is specified by UML diagrams.

Contextual instance
An instance of the contextual type of an OCL expression.

Contextual type
The type of the object for which an OCL expression will be evaluated.

Contract
A description of the services that are provided by an object using pre- and post-conditions.

Derivation rule
A rule that specifies the value of a derived element.

Derived class
A class whose features can be derived completely from already existing (base) classes and other derived classes.

Design by contract
A way of specifying software by describing the contract of each component or class explicitly, using pre- and postconditions.

Diagram
A visible rendering of (a part of) a model.

Dynamic multiplicity
The multiplicity of an association is dynamic, when it is determined based on another value in the system.

Features
The attributes, operations, and associations that are defined for a type.

Guard
A condition on a transition in a statechart.

Invariant
An invariant is a boolean expression attached to a type that states a condition that must always be met by all instances of the type for which it is defined.

Iterator variable
A variable that is used within the body of a loop expression to indicate the element of the collection for which the body is being calculated.

Language
A clearly defined way to model (parts of) a system. A definition of a language always consists of a syntax definition and a semantics definition.

Metamodel
A description or definition of a well-defined language. Equivalent to **metalanguage**.

Model
A consistent, coherent set of model elements with features and restrictions.

Model Driven Architecture
A framework for software development in which the process is driven by the automated transformation of platform-independent models into platform-specific models.

Model-driven software development
The process of developing software using different models on different levels of abstraction with (automated) transformations between these models.

Model repository
The storage of all model elements in an automated tool.

Navigation
Accessing objects different from the contextual instance using associations. Also, the association end through which a contextual instance may access another object.

Object type
A type that has reference-based identity.

Optional multiplicity
The multiplicity of an association is optional when its lowest bound is zero.

Platform
A set of software pieces implemented with a specific technology on specific hardware, and/or specific hardware pieces that constitute the execution environment of a system.

Platform-independent model
A model containing no details that have meaning only within a specific platform.

Platform-specific model
A model containing details which have meaning only within a specific platform.

Postcondition
An expression attached to an operation that must be true at the moment when the operation has just ended its execution.

Precondition
An expression attached to an operation that must be true at the moment when the operation is going to be executed.

Protocol interpretation of statecharts
A manner to understand statecharts in which every event, action, and activity is mapped to an operation of the class for which the statechart is defined. See also *real-time interpretation of statecharts.*

Query operation
An operation that has no side effects.

Real-time interpretation of statecharts
A manner to understand statecharts in which one single process executes the transitions by taking an event from an input queue and disposing it as specified by the statechart.

Reference-based identity
A type has reference-based identity when two references are considered to be unequal when the instances they refer to are not the same, even when all values held by both instances are the same.

Semantics
A definition of the meaning of models that are well-formed according to a syntax of a specific language.

Standard type
A type predefined in the OCL language, i.e., a type that is not defined by the user and cannot be altered by the user.

Syntax
A set of rules that defines which models are well-formed in a specific language.

System
A part of the world that is the subject of reasoning.

Transformation
A transformation is the generation of a model based on another model and a set of transformation rules, while preserving the meaning of the source model in the target model insofar as this meaning can be expressed in both models.

Type
A term used in this book to indicate either a class, a datatype, an interface, or a component.

Type conformance
Indicates whether an instance of one type can be substituted for an instance of another type. If so, the first type confoms to the second type.

UML profile
A language definition (a metamodel) based on the UML metamodel, with extra rules and a mapping of the language concepts to the UML syntax.

User-defined type
A model element defined in a UML diagram that represents an instance or set of instances—usually a class, datatype, component, or interface.

Value-based identity
A type has value-based identity when two references are considered to be equal when all values held by the instances they refer to are the same.

Value type
A type that has value-based identity.

OCL Grammar Rules

This appendix describes the grammar for OCL context declarations and expressions. This section is taken from [OCL03], which is the part of the UML 2.0 OMG standard that defines OCL. A free version of the Octopus tool, which implements this grammar, is available from the Klasse Objecten Web site: www.klasse.nl/ocl.

The grammar description uses the EBNF syntax, in which | means a choice, ? means optionality, * means zero or more times, and + means one or more times. In the description, the syntax for lexical tokens is not made explicit. Instead, it is indicated by <String>. This enables developers to use the grammar together with different natural language alphabets.

B.1 EBNF RULES FOR CONTEXT DECLARATION

```
packageDeclarationCS ::=
      'package' pathNameCS contextDeclCS* 'endpackage'
    | contextDeclCS*
```

```
contextDeclarationCS ::=
      attrOrAssocContextCS
    | classifierContextDeclCS
    | operationContextDeclCS
```

```
attrOrAssocContextCS ::=
    'context' pathNameCS '::' simpleName':' typeCS initOrDerValueCS
```

```
initOrDerValueCS[1] ::=
      'init'   ':'  OclExpression initOrDerValueCS?
    | 'derive' ':'  OclExpression initOrDerValueCS?
```

```
classifierContextDeclCS ::= 'context' pathNameCS invOrDefCS
```

```
invOrDefCS ::=
        'inv' (simpleNameCS)? ':' OclExpressionCS invOrDefCS
      | 'def' (simpleNameCS)? ':' defExpressionCS invOrDefCS
```

```
defExpressionCS ::=
        VariableDeclarationCS '=' OclExpression
      | operationCS '=' OclExpression
```

```
operationContextDeclCS ::= 'context' operationCS prePostOrBodyDeclCS
```

```
prePostOrBodyDeclCS ::=
        'pre' (simpleNameCS)? ':' OclExpressionCS prePostOrBodyDeclCS?
      | 'post' (simpleNameCS)? ':' OclExpressionCS prePostOrBodyDeclCS?
      | 'body' (simpleNameCS)? ':' OclExpressionCS prePostOrBodyDeclCS?
```

```
operationCS ::=
        pathNameCS '::' simpleNameCS '(' parametersCS? ')' ':' typeCS?
      | simpleNameCS '(' parametersCS? ')' ':' typeCS?
```

```
parametersCS ::= VariableDeclarationCS (',' parametersCS )?
```

B.2 EBNF RULES FOR EXPRESSION

```
OclExpressionCS ::=
            PropertyCallExpCS
          | VariableExpCS
          | LiteralExpCS
          | LetExpCS
          | OclMessageExpCS
          | IfExpCS
```

```
VariableExpCS ::= simpleNameCS
```

```
simpleNameCS ::= <String>
```

```
pathNameCS ::= simpleNameCS ('::' pathNameCS )?
```

```
LiteralExpCS ::=
            EnumLiteralExpCS
          | CollectionLiteralExpCS
          | TupleLiteralExpCS
          | PrimitiveLiteralExpCS
```

```
EnumLiteralExpCS ::= pathNameCS '::' simpleNameCS
```

```
CollectionLiteralExpCS ::= CollectionTypeIdentifierCS
                           '{' CollectionLiteralPartsCS? '}'
```

```
CollectionTypeIdentifierCS ::=
            'Set'
          | 'Bag'
          | 'Sequence'
          | 'OrderedSet'
          | 'Collection'
```

```
CollectionLiteralPartsCS = CollectionLiteralPartCS
                           ( ',' CollectionLiteralPartsCS )?
```

```
CollectionLiteralPartCS ::=
            CollectionRangeCS
          | OclExpressionCS
```

```
CollectionRangeCS ::= OclExpressionCS '..' OclExpressionCS
```

```
PrimitiveLiteralExpCS ::=
            IntegerLiteralExpCS
          | RealLiteralExpCS
          | StringLiteralExpCS
          | BooleanLiteralExpCS
```

```
TupleLiteralExpCS ::= 'Tuple' '{' variableDeclarationListCS '}'
```

```
IntegerLiteralExpCS ::= <String>
```

```
RealLiteralExpCS ::= <String>
```

```
StringLiteralExpCS ::= ''' <String> '''
```

```
BooleanLiteralExpCS ::=
            'true'
          | 'false'
```

```
PropertyCallExpCS ::=
            ModelPropertyCallExpCS
          | LoopExpCS
```

```
LoopExpCS ::=
            IteratorExpCS
          | IterateExpCS
```

```
IteratorExpCS ::=
            OclExpressionCS '->' simpleNameCS
                    '(' (VariableDeclarationCS,
                        (',' VariableDeclarationCS)? '|' )?
                        OclExpressionCS
                    ')'
            | OclExpressionCS '.' simpleNameCS '('argumentsCS?')'
            | OclExpressionCS '.' simpleNameCS
            | OclExpressionCS '.' simpleNameCS ('[' argumentsCS ']')?
```

```
IterateExpCS ::= OclExpressionCS '->' 'iterate'
                '(' (VariableDeclarationCS ';')?
                    VariableDeclarationCS '|'
                    OclExpressionCS
                ')'
```

```
VariableDeclarationCS ::= simpleNameCS (':' typeCS)?
                            ( '=' OclExpressionCS )?
```

```
typeCS ::=
            pathNameCS
          | collectionTypeCS
          | tupleTypeCS
```

```
collectionTypeCS ::= collectionTypeIdentifierCS '(' typeCS ')'
```

```
tupletypeCS ::= 'TupleType' '(' variableDeclarationListCS? ')'
```

```
ModelPropertyCallExpCS ::=
            OperationCallExpCS
          | AttributeCallExpCS
          | NavigationCallExpCS
```

```
OperationCallExpCS ::=
            OclExpressionCS simpleNameCS OclExpressionCS
          | OclExpressionCS '->' simpleNameCS '(' argumentsCS? ')'
          | OclExpressionCS '.' simpleNameCS '(' argumentsCS? ')'
          | simpleNameCS '(' argumentsCS? ')'
          | OclExpressionCS '.' simpleNameCS isMarkedPreCS
                                            '(' argumentsCS? ')'
          | simpleNameCS isMarkedPreCS '(' argumentsCS? ')'
          | pathNameCS '(' argumentsCS? ')'
          | simpleNameCS OclExpressionCS
```

```
AttributeCallExpCS ::=
          OclExpressionCS '.' simpleNameCS isMarkedPreCS?
        | simpleNameCS isMarkedPreCS?
        | pathNameCS
```

```
NavigationCallExpCS ::= AssociationEndCallExpCS
        | AssociationClassCallExpCS
```

```
AssociationEndCallExpCS ::= (OclExpressionCS '.')? simpleNameCS
                                ('[' argumentsCS ']')? isMarkedPreCS?
```

```
AssociationClassCallExpCS ::=
          OclExpressionCS '.' simpleNameCS
                ('[' argumentsCS ']')? isMarkedPreCS?
        | simpleNameCS
                ('[' argumentsCS ']')? isMarkedPreCS?
```

```
isMarkedPreCS ::= '@' 'pre'
```

```
argumentsCS ::= OclExpressionCS ( ',' argumentsCS )?
```

```
LetExpCS ::= 'let' VariableDeclarationCS
                LetExpSubCS
```

```
LetExpSubCS ::=
          ',' VariableDeclarationCS LetExpSubCS
        | 'in' OclExpressionCS
```

```
OclMessageExpCS ::=
          OclExpressionCS '^^'
              simpleNameCS '(' OclMessageArgumentsCS? ')'
        | OclExpressionCS '^'
              simpleNameCS '(' OclMessageArgumentsCS? ')'
```

```
OclMessageArgumentsCS ::= OclMessageArgCS (',' OclMessageArgumentsCS)?
```

```
OclMessageArgCS ::=
          '?' (':' typeCS)?
        | OclExpressionCS
```

```
IfExpCS ::= 'if'   OclExpression
                'then' OclExpression
                'else' OclExpression
                'endif'
```

AttributeDefinitionCS ::= 'attr' VariableDeclarationListCS

OperationDefinitionListCS ::= 'oper' OperationListCS

OperationListCS ::= OperationDefinitionCS (',' OperationListCS)

OperationDefinitionCS ::= 'simpleNameCS '(' parametersCS? ')'
                                  ':' typeCS ('=' OclExpresionCS)?

---

parametersCS ::= variableDeclarationCS (',' parametersCS)?

A Business Modeling Syntax for OCL

This appendix describes an alternative syntax for OCL expressions, one that is easier for business modelers. Note that this syntax is not standardized.

The Octopus tool, already mentioned in Appendix B, is able to transform the standard OCL syntax to this one. The tool is available from the Klasse Objecten Web site: www.klasse.nl/ocl.

C.1 INTRODUCTION

In the past, objections have been raised about the syntax of OCL. Some find it too difficult, others find it too different from mathematical languages. As it is, the OCL standard separates the concepts in the language from the concrete syntax used. This means that alternative concrete syntaxes can be made available. OCL expressions written in such an alternative syntax have exactly the same meaning as expressions written in the standard syntax. To give an example and demonstrate the feasibility of this approach, a syntax has been devised that is aimed at the business modeler.

The alternative syntax, from here on called the business modeling (BM) syntax, resembles the outward appearance of SQL, but supports all of the concepts in OCL. The main difference between the official syntax and the business modeling syntax is the notation for the predefined operations on collections and for the predefined iterators (loop expressions). Another difference is the absence of the implicit *collect*. Every *collect* operation needs to be explicitly stated. To give you a first feel for the syntax, one of the expressions from Chapter 2 ("OCL By Example") is shown here in the business modeling syntax:

```
context Customer
inv: size of programs = size of
        select i: CustomerCard from cards where i.valid = true
```

In the standard OCL syntax, this would be

```
context Customer
inv: programs->size() = cards->select( i.valid = true )
```

All examples given in this appendix are based on the R&L example from Chapter 2 ("OCL By Example"). As a convenience, we repeat the diagram for the R&L example in Figure C-1.

C.2 INFORMAL DEFINITION

As indicated in the previous section, the main difference between the standard syntax and the business modeling syntax lies in the predefined iterator expressions and the predefined collection operations. The following sections explain the alternative syntax for these two items. The syntax for the other language concepts remains largely the same as the standard syntax. The small number of differences are given in Section C.2.3.

C.2.1 Iterators

Every OCL iterator (loop expression) has the following format according to the standard syntax:

```
<source> ->iterator( <iters> | <body> )
```

The terms between the < > brackets serve as placeholders, and *iterator* stands for the name of the iterator from the Standard Library. The placeholder <source> indicates the collection over which to iterate, <iters> stands for the iterator variables, and <body> stands for the body parameter of the iterator.

In the BM syntax, each iterator has its own specialized format. Take for example the *select* iterator. Intuitively, one would say that one selects a thing or things from a set, taking into account any criteria. The BM syntax reflects this manner of speaking, as shown in the following expression, written in the context of *LoyaltyProgram*:

```
select pp: ProgramPartner from partners
    where pp.numberOfCustomers > 1000
```

The corresponding standard syntax is

```
partners->select(pp | pp.numberOfCustomers > 1000)
```

The *reject* and *any* iterators are written in a similar fashion, using the keywords *reject* and *selectAny*, respectively.

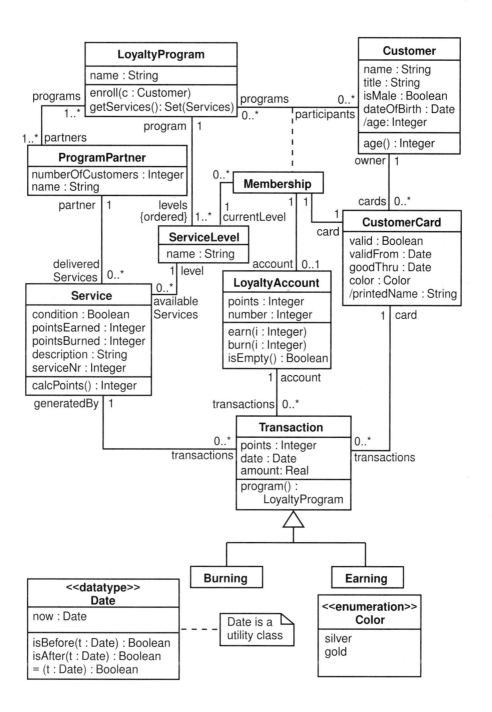

Figure C-1 *The Royal and Loyal model*

The following expression, again in the context of *LoyaltyProgram*, is an example of the BM syntax for the *collect* iterator:

```
collect p.deliveredServices using p: ProgramPartner
    from partners
```

It is built according to the intuition that one collects a thing (or things) from a set. To indicate the item to be collected, you may use a reference to an iterator variable, whose name and type are given after the keyword *using*. The *collectNested* iterator is written in the same manner, using the keyword *collectNested*.

The BM syntax for the *exists* and *one* iterator are built on the intuition that one asks whether an element exists in a set, given some criteria:

```
context CustomerCard
inv: exists t: Transaction in transactions
    where t.date.isBefore( Date::now )

context CustomerCard
inv: existsOne t: Transaction in transactions
    where t.date.isBefore( Date::now )
```

There still remains the *forAll*, *sortedBy*, and *isUnique* iterators. Examples of the BM syntax for these iterators are as follows (all written in the context *Customer*):

```
forall c: CustomerCard in cards isTrue c.valid

sort cards using c: CustomerCard by c.goodThru

isUnique c.color using c: CustomerCard in cards
```

In Table C-1, you can find the general description of the alternative syntax for each iterator using the placeholders <source>, <iters>, and <body>. As in the standard syntax, the iterator variables may be omitted. In that case, the corresponding keyword is omitted as well. For instance:

```
forall cards isTrue valid

sort cards by goodThru

isUnique color in cards
```

The more general *iterate* expression is defined in the standard syntax as:

```
<source> ->iterate( <iters> ; <result> = <initialValue> | <body> )
```

Again, the placeholder <source> indicates the collection over which to iterate; <iters> stands for the iterator varables; and <body> stands for the body of the iterator. Additionally, there are the placeholders <result> and <initialValue>. The first stands for the result variable name and type declaration. The second holds the initial value of the result variable.

The general description of the alternative syntax for the *iterate* expression is included in Table C-1. An example is the following invariant, which is equal to the expression *transactions.points->sum() > 0*:

```
context CustomerCard
inv: iterate t: Transaction over transactions
            result myResult : Integer
            initialValue 0
            nextValue myResult + points > 0
```

Table C-1 *Business modeling syntax for predefined iterators*

Iterator	Business Modeling Syntax
any	select any <iters> from <source> where <body>
collect	collect <body> using <iters> from <source>
collect nested	collect nested <body> using <iters> from <source>
exists	exists <iters> in <source> where <body>
forall	forall <iters> in <source> isTrue <body>
isunique	isUnique <body> using <iters> in <source>
iterate	iterate <iters> over <source> result <result> initial value <initialvalue> next value <body>
one	exists one <iters> in <source> where <body>
reject	reject <iters> from <source> where <body>
select	select <iters> from <source> where <body>
sortedby	sort <source> with <iters> by <body>

C.2.2 Collection Operations

According to the standard syntax, collection operations have the following format:

```
<source> -> operator( <arg1>, <arg2> )
```

Again, we use placeholders to indicate parts of the expression. The placeholder <source> indicates the collection over which to iterate. The <arg1> and <arg2> stand for the arguments of the operation, which are both optional. The term *operator* stands for the name of the collection operation from the Standard Library.

All collection operations with no arguments are written as a keyword followed by the collection to which they are applied. The keyword is usually the equivalent of the operation name. The following expressions in the context *Customer* are examples of the BM syntax for collection operations with no arguments:

```
sizeOf cards
isEmpty programs
asSequence cards
lastOf asSequence cards
```

The BM syntax for collection operations with one argument uses an extra keyword next to the operation name. For example, the *including* operation is written using the keywords *is* and *includedIn*:

```
is self includedIn
    collect c.owner using c: CustomerCard from cards
```

The *union* operation uses the keywords *unionOf* and *with*:

```
unionOf
    select c: CustomerCard from cards where c.valid
with
    select c: CustomerCard from cards where not c.valid
```

The BM syntax for collection operations with two arguments uses two extra keywords next to the operation name. One of the keywords separates the arguments. For example, the *insertAt* operation is written using the keywords *insert*, *at*, and *in*:

```
insert self at 3 in
    asSequence
        collect c.owner using c: CustomerCard from cards
```

In Table C-2, you can find the general description of the alternative syntax for each collection operation using the common placeholders.

Table C-2 *Business modeling syntax of collection operations*

Operation	Business Modeling Syntax
append	append \<arg1> to \<source>
asBag	asBag \<source>
asOrderedSet	asOrderedSet \<source>
asSequence	asSequence \<source>
asSet	asSet \<source>
at	at \<arg1> from \<source>
count	count \<arg1> in \<source>
excludes	is \<arg1> notIncludedIn \<source>
excludesAll	isAllOf \<arg1> notIncludedIn \<source>
excluding	exclude \<arg1> from \<source>
first	firstOf \<source>
flatten	flatten \<source>
includes	is \<arg1> includedIn \<source>
includesAll	isAllOf \<arg1> includedIn \<source>
including	include \<arg1> in \<source>
indexof	index of \<arg1> from \<source>
insertAt	insert \<arg1> at \<arg2> in \<source>
intersection	intersection \<arg1> with \<source>
isEmpty	isEmpty \<source>
last	lastOf \<source>
notEmpty	notEmpty \<source>
prepend	prepend \<arg1> to \<source>
size	sizeOf \<source>
subsequence	subsequence \<arg1> to \<arg2> of \<source>
sum	sumOf \<source>
symmetricDifference	symmetricDifference \<arg1> with \<source>
union	unionOf \<arg1> with \<source>

C.2.3 Other Differences

The local variable definition (*let* expression) is one of the expressions that is written slightly differently in the BM syntax. As usual, the difference lies in the use of keywords. The equal sign used to provide the value of the variable is changed into the keyword *be*, as shown in the following example:

```
context LoyaltyProgram
inv: let noc: Integer be
        collect numberOfCustomers from partners
    in forall pp: ProgramPartner in partners isTrue noc >= 10.000
```

Another difference between the standard and BM syntax is the keyword indicating the value of a feature at precondition time. In the standard syntax, it is written as *@pre*; in the BM syntax it is written as *atPre*, as shown here:

```
context Company::hireEmployee(p : Person)
post: employees = include p in employees atPre and
        stockprice() = stockprice atPre + 10
```

The last difference is the notation of the *isSent* and *message* operators. In the standard syntax they are written as ^ and ^^ respectively. In the BM syntax the keywords *isSentTo* and *sentTo* are used, and the order of target and message is switched, as shown in the following examples:

```
context File::save()
post: forAll b: Builder in self.project.builders
        isTrue incrementalBuild() isSentTo b
```

```
context Subject::hasChanged()
post:   let messages : Sequence(OclMessage) be
                collect update(? : Integer, ? : Integer) sentTo obs
                using obs
                from observers
        in forAll m in messages isTrue m.i <= m.j
```

C.3 SOME REMARKS ON THE RESEMBLANCE TO SQL

Although the BM syntax resembles the syntax of SQL, there are important differences between SQL and OCL. The main difference is that SQL statements work on complete tables. OCL expressions always take a single object as starting point. They work on what is visible from that object.

A common mistake is using the OCL *select* operation in the same manner as a SQL *select* statement. There is an important difference between the two. An OCL *select* operation results in a proper subset of the collection to which it was applied.

A SQL *select* statement does not result in a subset of the records in the table it is working on. In OCL terminology, it collects values that are visible from the records in the table. Assume, for the sake of the argument, that the R&L diagram in Figure C-1 represents a database schema. The following SQL statement would result in a list of dates:

```
SELECT goodThru FROM CustomerCard WHERE valid = true
```

The OCL equivalent of this SQL statement would be

```
collect cc.goodThru using cc: CustomerCard
from select cc: CustomerCard from allInstances of CustomerCard
    where cc.valid = true
```

C.4 MORE ELABORATE EXAMPLES

This section contains some extensive examples of the use of the BM syntax. An OCL expression is taken and written in the alternative notation. For sake of clarity, the keywords used in the BM notation are written with capital letters.

The expression

```
context Customer
inv: programs->size() = cards->select( valid = true )->size()
```

becomes

```
context Customer
inv: size of programs = size of
    select i: CustomerCard from cards where i.valid = true
```

The expression

```
context LoyaltyProgram
inv: partners.deliveredServices->forAll(
        pointsEarned = 0 and pointsBurned = 0 )
      implies Membership.account->isEmpty()
```

becomes

```
context LoyaltyProgram
inv: forall s : Service in
        collect p.deliveredServices
        using p : ProgramPartner from partners
      is true ( ( pointsEarned= 0 and pointsBurned= 0 )
```

```
                    implies isempty
                         collect account
                         using l: LoyaltyAccount from membership )
```

The expression

```
context LoyaltyProgram
def: getServices(levelName: String)
      = Servicelevel->select( name = levelName ).availableServices
```

becomes

```
context LoyaltyProgram
def: getServices(String levelName)
      = collect s.availableServices
        using s: ServiceLevel from
              select sl: ServiceLevel
              from Servicelevel
              where sl.name = levelName
```

The expression

```
context ProgramPartner
inv: deliveredServices.transactions
        ->select( isOclType( Burning ) )
              ->collect( points )->sum() < 10,000
```

becomes

```
context ProgramPartner
inv: sum of
      collect t.points
      using t : Transaction from
        select b: Transaction from
            collect s.transactions
            using s : Service from deliveredServices
        where b.isOclType( Burning ) < 10,000
```

Example Implementation

This appendix provides an example of the implementation of OCL expressions as explained in Chapter 4. The class *CustomerCard*, together with all OCL expressions given as examples in this book, is implemented by the following Java code:

```java
package royalAndLoyal;

import java.util.HashSet;
import java.util.Iterator;
import java.util.Set;

public class CustomerCard {

/******************************************************************
 *   Attributes, and their get and set operations
 *
 ******************************************************************/
boolean valid = true;     // implements initial value
                          // definition from page 24
Date validFrom;
Date goodThru;
Color color;

public void setValid(boolean v) {
  valid = v;
}

public boolean getValid() {
  return valid;
}

public void setValidFrom(Date d) {
  validFrom = d;
}
```

```java
public Date getValidFrom() {
  return validFrom;
}

public void setGoodThru(Date d) {
  goodThru = d;
}

public Date getGoodThru() {
  return goodThru;
}

public void setColor(Color c) {
  color = c;
}

public Color getColor() {
  return color;
}

/****************************************************************
 *   Associations, and their get and set operations
 *
 ****************************************************************/
Customer owner;
HashSet transactions = new HashSet();  // implements initial
                                       // value definition
                                       // Set{} from page 112
Membership membership;

public void setOwner(Customer c) {
  owner = c;
}

public Customer getOwner() {
  return owner;
}

public void addTransaction(Transaction t) {
  transactions.add(t);
}

public HashSet getTransactions() {
  return transactions;
}

public void setMembership(Membership m) {
```

```
    membership = m;
}

public Membership getMembership() {
  return membership;
}

/****************************************************************
 *   Derived attributes, and their get and set operations
 *
 ****************************************************************/
/* implements from page 25:
   context CustomerCard::printedName
   derive: owner.title.concat(' ').concat(owner.name)
*/
String getPrintedName() {
  return owner.getTitle() + " " + owner.getName();
}

/* implements from page 112:
   context CustomerCard::myLevel : ServiceLevel
   derive: Membership.currentLevel
*/
ServiceLevel getMyLevel() {
  return membership.getCurrentLevel();
}

/****************************************************************
 *   Invariants
 *   Operations to be called when an invariant needs to be checked
 *
 ****************************************************************/
/* implements from page 27:
    inv: validFrom.isBefore(goodThru)
 */
boolean invCorrectValidFrom() {
  return validFrom.isBefore(goodThru);
}

/* implements from page 28:
    inv: owner.age >= 18
*/
boolean invCorrectAge() {
  return owner.age >= 18;
}

/* implements from page 36:
    inv: let correctDate : Boolean =
```

```
                        self.validFrom.isBefore(Date::now) and
                        self.goodThru.isAfter(Date::now)
                in
            if valid then
                correctDate = false
            else
                correctDate = true
            endif
    */
    boolean invValidMatchesDates() {
            boolean correctDate =
                    this.validFrom.isBefore(Date.now) &&
                    this.goodThru.isAfter(Date.now);
            if (valid) {
              return correctDate == false;
            } else {
              return correctDate == true;
            }
    }


    /* implements from page 130:
       inv: goodThru.isAfter( Date::now )
    */
    boolean invCorrectGoodThru() {
      return goodThru.isBefore( Date.now );
    }


    /* implements from page 131:
       inv: self.owner.dateOfBirth.isBefore( Date::now )
    */
    boolean invCorrectDateOfBirth() {
      return this.getOwner().getDateOfBirth().isBefore( Date.now );
    }


    /* implements from page 131:
       inv: self.owner.programs->size() > 0
    */
    boolean invCorrectNumberOfPrograms() {
      return this.getOwner().getPrograms().size() > 0;
    }


    /* implements from page 149:
       inv: self.transactions->select( points > 100 )->notEmpty()
    */
    boolean invCorrectNrHighTransactions() {
      boolean result = false;
      Iterator it = this.getTransactions().iterator();
      Set selectResult = new HashSet();
```

```
  while( it.hasNext() ){
    Transaction t = (Transaction) it.next();
    if (t.getPoints() > 100 ) {
      selectResult.add( t );
    }
  }
  result = ! selectResult.isEmpty();
  return result;
}

/* implements from page 184, using different OCL syntax:
  inv: exists t: Transaction in transactions
     where t.date.isBefore( Date::now )
*/
boolean invCorrectDateOfTransactions() {
  return this.getOwner().getDateOfBirth().isBefore( Date.now );
}

/* implements from page 184, using different OCL syntax:
  inv: iterate t: Transaction over transactions
              result myResult : Integer
              initialValue 0
              nextValue myResult + points  > 0
*/
boolean invCorrectPoints() {
  Iterator it = transactions.iterator();
  int myResult = 0;
  while( it.hasNext() ) {
    Transaction t = (Transaction) it.next();
    myResult = myResult + t.getPoints();
  }
  return myResult > 0;
}


/* convenience operation that checks all invariants
 * could also be implemented to return an error code,
 * exception, or error message
 */
boolean checkAllInvariants() {
  return invCorrectValidFrom()&
         invCorrectAge() &&
         invValidMatchesDates() &&
         invCorrectGoodThru() &&
         invCorrectDateOfBirth() &&
         invCorrectNumberOfPrograms() &&
         invCorrectNrHighTransactions() &&
         invCorrectDateOfTransactions() &&
```

```
              invCorrectPoints();
    }

    /****************************************************************
     *   Definitions
     *
     ****************************************************************/
    /* implements from page 113:
       context CustomerCard::getTransactions(from : Date, until: Date )
                                     : Set(Transaction)
       body: transactions->select( date.isAfter( from ) and
                              date.isBefore( until ) )
    */
    Set getTransactions( Date from, Date until ) {
      Set result = new HashSet();
      Iterator it = this.getTransactions().iterator();
      while( it.hasNext() ){
        Transaction t = (Transaction) it.next();
       if (t.getDate().isAfter(from) && t.getDate().isBefore(until) ){
          result.add( t );
        }
      }
      return result;
    }

    /* implements from page 111:
       context CustomerCard
       def: getTotalPoints( d: Date ) : Integer =
             transactions->select( date.isAfter(d) ).points->sum()
    */
    int getTotalPoints( Date d ) {
      int result = 0;
      Iterator it = this.getTransactions().iterator();
      while( it.hasNext() ){
        Transaction t = (Transaction) it.next();
        if (t.getDate().isAfter(d) ) {
          result = result + t.points;
        }
      }
      return result;
    }

    } // end class CustomerCard
```

Appendix E

Differences Between OCL Versions 1.1 and 2.0

The previous edition of this book, which appeared in 1999, described OCL version 1.1. This edition describes OCL version 2.0. This appendix lists the differences between both versions of the OCL standard.

E.1 SYNTAX CHANGES

E.1.1 Context Declaration

In version 1.1, there was no syntax for declaring the context of an expression; there was only the convention to underline the classname (for invariants) or the operation name (for pre- and postconditions) to indicate the context. In version 2.0, the context declaration is formalized. A new syntax is provided using the keyword *context*, and several different keywords indicate how the expression should be interpreted, e.g., *inv* and *derive*.

E.1.2 Enumerations and Class Attributes and Operations

The syntax for specifying enumeration types has changed from UML 1.1 to UML 2.0. In the current version, enumeration types are specified more or less like other types are denoted. In correspondence, the OCL syntax for using enumeration values has been changed. An enumeration value in OCL version 2.0 must be written as follows:

```
EnumTypeName::EnumLiteralValue
```

The syntax for using class attributes and operations has also changed. They must be prefixed by the classname and two colons, as in the following:

```
ClassName::StaticAttribute
```

E.1.3 Missing Rolenames and Using Association Classes

In version 1.1, you indicated an association for which the rolename is missing by stating the classname, starting with a lowercase letter. This is changed because it cannot be done in non-ascii typefaces. The syntax in version 2.0 is simply the classname as is.

The syntax for accessing an instance of an association class is likewise adapted.

E.1.4 Operations

Contrary to version 1.1, all predefined aspects are defined as operations and must therefore be written using brackets.

E.2 NEW TYPES

OCL verson 2.0 includes a number of newly defined types. As a new form of collection, the *OrderedSet* type is included. Furthermore, tuples and tuple types may be used, and there is an explicit type for a very special value, the undefined value. This type conforms to all other types.

E.3 EXTRA PREDEFINED OPERATIONS

Note a large number of additional predefined operations on collections:

- *collectNested*
- *flatten*
- *excludes*
- *excludesAll*
- *insertAt*
- *indexOf*
- *any*
- *one*
- *isUnique*
- *sortedBy*

As a convenience, extra operations are defined; for example, *asSet()* can be called on a set instance, and so on. Furthermore, you can convert a set or a bag to a sequence or ordered set using the *sortedBy* operation. This operation results in a sequence with a certain order, instead of a random sequence as is the case with the *asSequence* operation.

E.4 NEW OPTIONS IN POSTCONDITIONS

Completely new in version 2.0 is the option to specify that an object has sent messages to other objects during the execution of an operation. The general syntax is: `calledObject^calledOperation(params)`. To support this, a new *OclMessage* type has been defined, together with a number of convenience operations:

- *isSent*
- *isSignalSent*
- *isOperationCall*
- *hasReturned*
- *result*

Another aspect that can be examined in a postcondition is whether or not an object was created during the execution of the operation. The predefined operation *oclIsNew* returns true if the object was not in existence at precondition time.

E.5 OTHER CHANGES

Note a number of other difference between version 1.1 and version 2.0:
- In version 1.1 you were able to specify constraints only. In version 2.0 you may use OCL expressions to specify not only constraints, but value specifications in general, for instance, an initial value, derivation rule, or operation body.
- A new construct called *Let* is added to OCL version 2.0. This allows for the definition of local variables within constraints.
- The operation *oclType* for *OclAny* has been removed, because objects may have multiple types.
- States can be referenced from OCL. The operation *oclInState()* is added to check whether an object is in a certain state.
- Use of user-defined infix operators (+, -, *, /, etc.) is defined.
- The precedence rules have been extended and changed.
- One may use /* and */ to indicate large comments.
- One may use packaging expressions to group expressions together.
- One can explicitly state the type of the elements of a collection.

Bibliography

[Akehurst01] D. H. Akehurst and B. Bordbar, *On Querying UML Data Models with OCL*, <<UML>> 2001 - The Unified Modeling Language, Modeling Languages, Concepts and Tools, 4th International Conference, Toronto, Canada, 2001.

[Balsters03] H. Balsters, *Modeling Database Views with Derived Classes in the UML/OCL-framework*, to appear in the proceedings of <<UML>> 2003 "Modeling Languages and Applications" October 20 - 24, 2003, San Francisco, California, USA.

[Blaha98] Michael Blaha and William Premerlani, *Object-Oriented Modeling and Design for Database Applications*, Prentice-Hall, 1998.

[Booch94] Grady Booch, *Object-Oriented Analysis and Design with Applications*, 2nd ed, Benjamin/Cummings, 1994.

[Booch99] Grady Booch, James Rumbaugh, and Ivar Jacobson, *The Unified Modeling Language User Guide*, Addison-Wesley, 1999.

[CMM95] Carnegie Mellon University/Software Engineering Institute, *The Capability Maturity Model: Guidelines for Improving the Software Process*, Addison-Wesley, 1995.

[Coleman94] Derek Coleman, P. Arnold, S. Bodoff, C. Dollin, H. Chilchrist, F. Hayes, and P. Jeremaes, *Object-Oriented Development: The Fusion Method*, Prentice-Hall, 1994.

[Cook94] Steve Cook and John Daniels, *Designing Object Systems—Object Oriented Modeling with Syntropy*, Prentice-Hall, 1994.

[D'Souza99] Desmond F. D'Souza and Alan C. Wills, *Objects, Components, and Frameworks with UML: The Catalysis Approach*, Addison-Wesley, 1999.

[EJB01] *UML/EJB Mapping specification*, Java Community Process Document JSR26, 2001.

[Eriksson00] Hans-Erik Eriksson and Magnus Penker, *Business Modeling with UML, Business Patterns at Work*, John Wiley & Sons, 2000.

[Fowler97] Martin Fowler, *UML Distilled: Applying the Standard Object Modeling Language*, Addison-Wesley, 1997.

[Graham95] Ian Graham, *Migrating to Object Technology*, Addison-Wesley, 1995.

[Jacobson99] Ivar Jacobson, Grady Booch, and James Rumbaugh, *The Unified Software Development Process*, Addison-Wesley, 1999.

[Kleppe03] Anneke Kleppe, Jos Warmer, and Wim Bast, *MDA Explained; The Model Driven Architecture: Practice and Promise*, Addison-Wesley, 2003.

[Liskov94] Barbara Liskov and Jeanette Wing, "A Behavioral Notion of Subtyping," *ACM Transactions on Programming Languages and Systems*, Vol. 16, No. 6, November 1994, pp. 1811–1841.

[Meyer85] Bertrand Meyer, "On Formalism in Specifications," *IEEE Software*, January 1985.

[Meyer88] Bertrand Meyer, *Object-Oriented Software Construction*, Prentice-Hall, 1988.

[Meyer91] Bertrand Meyer, "Design by Contract," in *Advances in Object-Oriented Software Engineering*, Prentice-Hall, 1991, pp. 1–50.

[Meyer92] Bertrand Meyer, "Applying Design by Contract," *IEEE Computer*, October 1992.

[OCL97] *Object Constraint Language Specification*, version 1.1, OMG document ad970808, 1997.

[OCL03] Response to the UML 2.0 OCL RfP, revision 1.6, OMG document ad2003-01-06.

[Richters01] Mark Richters, *A Precise Approach to Validating UML Models and OCL Constraints*, Logos Verlag Berlin, 2001.

[Rumbaugh91] James Rumbaugh, Michael Blaha, William Premelani, Frederick Eddy, and William Lorensen, *Object-Oriented Modeling and Design*, Prentice-Hall, 1991.

[Rumbaugh99] James Rumbaugh, Grady Booch, and Ivar Jacobson, *Unified Modeling Language Reference Manual*, Addison-Wesley, 1999.

[Selic94] Bran Selic, Garth Gullekson, and Paul T. Ward, *Real-Time Object-Oriented Modeling*, John Wiley & Sons, 1994.

[UML97] *UML 1.1 Specification*, OMG documents ad970802–ad0809, 1997.

[Waldén95] Kim Waldén and Jean-Marc Nerson, *Seamless Object-Oriented Software Architecture: Analysis and Design of Reliable Systems*, Prentice-Hall, 1995.

[Wirfs-Brock90] Rebecca Wirfs-Brock, Brian Wilkerson, and Lauren Wiener, *Designing Object-Oriented Software,* Prentice-Hall, 1990.

[Wordsworth92] J. Wordsworth, *Software Development with Z,* Addison-Wesley, Berkshire, 1992.

Index

Also Available from Addison-Wesley

MDA Explained
The Model Driven Architecture™: Practice and Promise

by Anneke Kleppe, Jos Warmer, and Wim Bast

0-321-19442-X
Paperback
192 pages
© 2003

Written by three members of OMG's MDA standardization committee, **MDA Explained** gives readers an inside look at the advantages of MDA and how they can be realized. This book begins with practical examples that illustrate the application of different types of models. It then shifts to a discussion at the meta-level, where developers will gain the knowledge necessary to define MDA tools.

Highlights of this book include:

• The MDA framework, including the Platform Independent Model (PIM) and Platform Specific Model (PSM)

• OMG standards and the use of UML

• MDA and Agile, Extreme Programming, and Rational Unified Process (RUP) development

• How to apply MDA, including PIM-to-PSM and PSM-to-code transformations, for relational, Enterprise JavaBean (EJB), and Web models

• Transformations, including controlling and tuning, traceability, incremental consistency, and their implications

• Metamodeling

• Relationships between different standards, including Meta Object Facility (MOF), UML, and Object Constraint Language (OCL)

The advent of MDA offers concrete ways to dramatically improve productivity, portability, interoperability, maintenance, and documentation. With this groundbreaking book, IT professionals can learn to tap this new framework to deliver enterprise systems most efficiently.